Green  Fields

ALSO BY BOB COWSER, JR.:

Why We're Here: New York Essayists on Living Upstate (ed.)

Dream Season: A Professor Joins America's Oldest Semi-Pro Football Team

Scorekeeping: Essays From Home

Green Fields

Crime, Punishment, & a Boyhood Between

BOB COWSER, JR.

unoPRESS

Printed in the USA

Library of Congress Control Number: 2010920787

ISBN 13: 978-1-60801-018-9

Cover photo courtesy of the State of Tennessee,
used by permission

Book & cover design by Kelcy D. Wilburn

UNOPRESS

University of New Orleans Publishing
Managing Editor, Bill Lavender
http://unopress.uno.edu

THE ENGAGED WRITERS SERIES
University of New Orleans Publishing
Managing Editor, Bill Lavender
http://unopress.uno.edu

Acknowledgments

This is a work of nonfiction, about people who actually lived (and live still) and things that actually happened. I want first to mention the work of reporters for publications like *The Jackson Sun*, *The Commercial Appeal* (Memphis), *The Tennessean* (Nashville), *Weakley County Press*, *The Daily Messenger* (Union City), and *The Nashville Scene* (especially Richard Urban), upon whose reporting and writing I have relied greatly in piecing my story together lo these three decades later. Theirs was, as they say, the first draft of this history, and I, as a sort of revisionist, am in their debt.

I should acknowledge, too, that my book, though based on these real events, is also a work of the imagination. That is not to say I have fabricated or invented a single detail but merely to accept that, as Joan Didion (patron saint of this book, to my mind) reminds in the introduction to 1979's *The White Album*, "we live entirely, especially if we are writers, by the imposition of a narrative line upon disparate images… the shifting phantasmagoria of our actual experience."

Didion may mean "imposition" in the most innocuous sense, as in the arrangement of printed matter to form a sequence of pages, but I suspect she intends its more conventional meaning, as in an unfair burden. The forging of this narrative is, again, a creative act; "we interpret what we see," says Didion, "look for the sermon in the suicide, for the social or moral lesson in the murder of five." And while I embrace the subjectivity of the project, I must acknowledge its violence, too. If my book offends, please pardon this imposition. My purpose has never been to do more harm or violence, simply to bear witness.

I want to thank so many who supported and encouraged me as I drafted this book: Macreena Doyle, Karl Schonberg, Caroline Breashears, Mary Hussmann, Sarah Gates, Liz Regosin and Natalia Singer at St. Lawrence University; Gary Clark, Jill Osier, and Asako Serizawa at the Vermont Studio Center; Alice Elliott Dark, Jan Freeman, LuAnn Keener, Craig Urquhart and Hubert Ho at the Virginia Center for the Creative Arts; Jill Christman,

Sonya Huber, Ruth Schwartz, Angie Estes, Kathy Winograd, Bob Root, Steve Harvey, Steve Haven, Dan Lehman and Sarah Wells at the Ashland University MFA Program; my students at St. Lawrence and Ashland Universities and at the Ray Brook Federal Correctional Institution and the Gouverneur (NY) Correctional Facility; Charlie Johnson, Stacy Bell McQuaide and Melissa Benton and all those associated with the Inside Out Prison Exchange Program around the country.

I should mention old friends from Martin, Tennessee, like Mike Dunn, DoRann Killebrew, Sky McCracken and David Nanney, who shared their memories of these events. Charlotte Stout was gracious enough to make time to talk to me one fall afternoon a few years ago. Special thanks to Susan Turner, chief clerk at the Tennessee Supreme Court building in Jackson, who allowed me access to all court records on more than one occasion.

I am grateful to the editors who published parts of this book in their magazines: Dinty Moore at *Brevity*, and Kristen Iversen, Wendy Sumner-Winter, and Mike Petrik with *The Pinch*. And to friends who talked to me about trying to make the book better, namely Robin Hemley, David Shields, Peter Campion, my agents Jane Dystel and Miriam Goderich.

As has become the routine, great friends Paul Graham and William Bradley read several drafts of the manuscript, and trusty copy editor Neal Burdick gave a final once-over. I am so fortunate to enjoy their continued collaboration. I cannot thank Bill Lavender at UNO Press enough for giving this book a home, or Steven Church for suggesting he consider doing so.

Finally, thanks to my families, the one I was born to in Tennessee and the one Candace and I have made here in New York. I drew great strength from their faith and trust in me to tell this story, and only hope I was worthy of it.

B.C.

Canton, NY
January 2010

Contents

The scene in the forest had become for me, without my knowing it, the foundation for the real story I am now trying to tell. The fragments, you see, had to be picked up slowly, long afterwards. The whole thing... was to me as I grew older like music heard from far off. The notes had to be picked up slowly, one at a time. Something had to be understood... I shall not try to emphasize the point. I am only trying to explain why I was dissastisfied then and have been ever since. I speak of that only that you may understand why I have been impelled to tell the simple story over again.

Sherwood Anderson, "Death in the Woods"

In Another Lifetime

'Twas in another lifetime, one of toil and blood...
Bob Dylan, "Shelter From the Storm"

Greenfield, Tennessee, a farm and factory town of 2,200 in the state's rural northwest corner, has never been more than a place between places, one in a long list of tiny hamlets merely to be passed through along kudzu-choked highways running south to Jackson and then Memphis, towns with names like Hornbeak and Frogjump and Bucksnort and Catfight and Skullbone. More than a century ago now a conductor on a southbound Illinois Central train offered Greenfield its name, noting the fields of winter wheat still green late in the year.

It was the railroad and not the nearby Mississippi River that was the prime mover in the delta land where I grew up. I hail from the slightly larger city of Martin, thirteen miles north up Highway 45 from Greenfield, named for tobacco plantation owner Colonel William Martin whose sons had donated land for the Illinois Central railroad bed. Engineer Casey Jones lived fifty miles south in Jackson at the time of his legendary 1903 wreck, his modest house there now a museum. The mosquitoes blamed for the 1878 Yellow Fever epidemic that felled 400 Martin residents and killed 52 (victims were quarantined post mortem in their own cemetery) arrived from New Orleans in Illinois Central boxcars.

On September 2, 1979, two members of the Weakley County Rescue Squad found the raped and murdered body of eight-year-old Cary Ann Medlin in one of the community's namesake green fields, not far from the railroad tracks. Cary had gone on a bike ride with her stepbrother Michael the evening before, gotten into a stranger's brown Gran Torino and disappeared. By the time they found her tiny body twenty hours later atop a trampled swath of chest-high weeds just off Bean Switch Road, a notorious lovers' lane, the corpse had begun to turn in the late summer heat.

Cary Medlin had been in my first grade class at the Martin Elementary School two years prior, both of us students of the venerable Mrs. Mary Agnes Thomason. Cary Ann's stepfather worked in those days on the assembly line at Goodyear Tire and Rubber in Union City, and before moving to Greenfield in the summer of '79 the family had lived for a time in the University Courts apartments, across the road from the hospital where her mother worked as a registered nurse. My family had lived at University Courts for a short while as well, just after my parents had moved to town to begin teaching at the small college there. Cary was a girl I knew, a playmate.

I remember hearing news of her murder and running to find my first-grade yearbook, hoping to fix her school photo in my mind so I wouldn't lose the memory of her face. I was as sad as a nine-year-old boy could be about the business. Still, the abduction and murder did not interrupt my childhood in the way one might imagine. Cary had violated that cardinal rule about talking to strangers, after all, and the Weakley County Sheriff's Department had the confessed killer, 23-year-old Robert Glen Coe of nearby McKenzie, in custody in the county courthouse in Dresden just three days later. Authorities had nabbed him in Huntingdon, Tennessee, boarding a Greyhound bus bound for Georgia under an assumed name, his hair blackened with what looked like shoe polish.

Not until 21 years after Cary's murder, long after I'd left Tennessee, after that lovers' lane had become a memory lane, did I begin to consider the murder's place in my childhood. As the state of Tennessee prepared to execute Coe for the Medlin murder, its first execution in forty years, I began to wonder about Bean Switch Road and what happened there and how I carried it with me all these years later. There are plenty of studies examining the effects of domestic and community violence on those children directly affected, raised at the flashpoint— they are withdrawn or hyperactive, prone to intrusive flashbacks. Many act out, relive traumatic events but as actors now rather than victims or bystanders. But there are no studies of the effects on those who stand at one or two removes from trauma's epicenter, a few rows away from that empty desk in third grade.

That first grade photo of Cary appeared over and over in the news in the months leading up to the Coe execution, along with another I found printed years before in the Nashville *Tennessean* and now reprinted as local newspapers re-capped the story: a shot of those rescue workers bent over the soybean plants, long-haired and t-shirted, hunting the girl's body. The latter photo didn't chill me so much as fascinate me. I sensed with strange excitement how the photo was some kind of emblem— the unmistakable heat, those men, something awful hidden just out of sight. "Images of the repulsive," writes Susan Sontag, "can also allure."

So the story has become one I have to tell. "Why a writer should be so egotistical as to have such feelings about a whole region and so crass as to express these feelings is a mystery," writes the novelist Peter Taylor, a fellow northwest Tennessean who grew up fifteen miles south of Greenfield in Trenton. "But nearly everything about art is a mystery," Taylor goes on, "and must ever be so."

Maybe a mystery is what this story is. The murder and execution certainly aren't *news* anymore. Both Medlin and Coe are as dead as they could be— Coe for almost ten years at this writing, Cary Ann for three decades. Yet it's not *history* either, at least not for me. My ten-year-old son Jackson used to like to curl up with his mother in his pre-school years and watch the 10 p.m. police dramas. He called them "figuring-out shows," realizing that figuring out who the bad guys are is the point of such murder mysteries. I want to treat this story as a murder mystery of another kind, not as a whodunit but as the sort of "detective story" William Kittredge describes in *Learning to Think*: a series of scenes witnessed by a figure (the author) trying to fathom their meaning, leading finally to some kind of recognition for both writer and reader.

After all, something has drawn you here. You want to know what it is the searchers seek among the ragweed and soybean plants— the tiny body, yes, but something more. Now this book lies open before you, each paragraph a stand of trees, a deep forest of wonder and darkness. Its mystery beckons.

Chapter 1:
End of Summer

I believe she's never gone away…

The Doobie Brothers, "What a Fool Believes"

Charlotte Stout remembers her chestnut-haired daughter Cary Ann Medlin, nearly nine years old, hurrying down the steps of her family's new A-frame home about 5:30 p.m. on the evening of September 1, 1979, wearing a little red Boswell's Harley Davidson t-shirt and red gym shorts.

"We're going riding," Cary announced.

Her seven-year-old stepbrother Michael followed closely on her heels. The two rode all the time since Cary had gotten a new bike for Christmas. Charlotte had thought the new bike too big for her little girl at first, but Cary was out of training wheels in just a few weeks. "Be back in thirty minutes," she called after the children. "The lasagna will be ready."

Cary Ann ran out the door barefoot, as usual, but because her mother fussed at her about wearing shoes on her bicycle the little girl had in hand a pair of wooden-soled sandals with a white leather strap which her mother saw her slip over the handlebars once she got outside. Cary Ann was mostly a good girl if a lackluster student at the Greenfield Elementary. "I tried to get her to learn her math," one teacher told her mother. "But I guess she knew what was really important." Michael Stout thought Cary Ann was a good big sister, even though she was a little bossy. The children set out for their

19

grandmother's house, one street over on Fairlane Drive. They were forbidden to ride off their block but often made this short trip in search of candy.

It was a warm, late summer evening in Greenfield, Tennessee, the temperature having climbed as high as ninety degrees earlier in the afternoon. Eight months pregnant and tired nearly all the time, Charlotte Stout had slept most of the day to beat the heat. But she was up now, preparing to work the night shift as an emergency room nurse at the Volunteer General Hospital fourteen miles north in Martin. Her younger half-sister Tina was over and the two had started to put supper on the table for Cary and Michael. Nineteen-year-old Tina planned to stay behind after Charlotte left for work to help Charlotte's husband, Mickey, watch the children. She'd lived with Mickey and Charlotte on and off since leaving home at eighteen and often helped with the children.

After Charlotte's marriage to Mickey Stout a couple of years before, the second for both, Charlotte had enrolled in nursing school at the branch of the University of Tennessee located in Martin, and the young family had lived for a time in University Courts, the married-student housing units there. Charlotte had since finished school and was now working full-time at the hospital, Mickey at the tire plant in Union City, and the Stouts had very recently moved into the new A-frame home Mickey and his father, Joe William Stout, had built at the dead end of Belair Drive in Greenfield. Cary Ann was adjusting to a new school and eagerly awaiting the birth of Mickey and Charlotte's first child together. She had picked out a bib for the new baby at a yard sale a few days before and tucked under her pillow a card addressed "To Momma and the Baby."

Mickey's stepmother, Maggie Lee Stout, was sitting in her living room watching some television when Cary Ann and Michael burst in. ("Soap operas?" the prosecutor asked her during Robert Glen Coe's murder trial in Memphis a few years later. "Country music," she told him.) Like her daughter-in-law, Maggie Lee was getting ready to go in to Martin to work. She and her husband, Joe, owned and operated "Maggie Lee's" night club on Highway 22. Mrs. Stout also sang and played keyboards for the house band, "Maggie Lee and the Percussions." Joe Stout was the band's drummer and manager, and in younger days they'd recorded with Sam Phillips in Memphis and toured extensively. Now they opened at the club a couple of nights a week, though Joe was no longer behind the drum kit, proprietor's duties having pulled him away. His son Mickey and the band he formed with his high-school buddies played "Maggie Lee's" from time to time, and when Mickey lost his job at Goodyear, Joe hired him to clean up around the club.

Maggie Stout told the children she had no candy and sent them back out into the evening. She heard the door close and roused herself to take a phone call. Maggie watched her grandchildren out her kitchen window as they walked their bikes across the lawn to Fairlane Drive. She saw a greasy-haired young man in a four-door brown on brown sedan pull up to Michael and Cary Ann, who were by now straddling their bikes in the street. The man had neck-length, brownish blonde hair, Maggie told police later, an ugly face.

The children spoke to the man in the car for several minutes. Early newspaper reports indicate he called the children— Cary at least— by name, though Michael Stout does not remember that. Maggie Stout could not hear what was said. She saw both children pointing back to the house, then saw the car start to pull away very slowly and watched her grandchildren begin to follow on their bicycles, noting the jacked up rear end of the sedan as its tail lights disappeared south down Fairlane. She got off the phone so she could get ready to go to the club. It was now a quarter to 6 p.m.

Michael Stout had seen the brown car follow him and his sister as they rode back and forth between his father's home and the Greenfield Primitive Baptist Church just down the street before it finally pulled up to them in front of Maggie Stout's home. The little boy says the man in the car asked if he was kin to Mickey Stout and if Cary was. He seemed to know Michael's father and was nice and not rough with the children. "I told him I was Mickey Stout's real son and Cary was his stepdaughter," Michael would later testify.

The man in the car asked the children to lead him back to the church parking lot on Evergreen Street, where Cary Ann got in the car with the stranger. In his confession, Robert Glen Coe says she promised to lead him to her stepfather, but Michael could not hear anything said between the man and his stepsister. The greasy-haired man finally called out from the car's open driver's side window and instructed Michael to wait at the church and guard the bikes while he and Cary went on their errand.

Retired octogenarian Herbert Clement (deaf in one ear and hard of hearing in the other, he told the court) was perhaps the last person other than her killer to see Cary Ann Medlin alive. From the front porch of his home a mile or so north of downtown Greenfield, Clement noticed the brown sedan pass his house headed into town. Some time after, around 6 p.m., he saw the car headed out of town again toward Bean Switch Road and noticed a little girl in the passenger seat whom he recognized from the sidewalks of downtown Greenfield as little Cary Ann Medlin. ("She knew more people than I did, the little chatterbox," her mother says.) Cary Ann sat between Clement and the driver, so the old man never got a look at the stranger behind the wheel.

*

Odd that what so many of the players in this drama remember about the day of Cary Ann's disappearance is soundless, a series of awful silent movies: Maggie Stout could not hear her grandchildren talking to the man in the brown car outside her kitchen window; young Michael Stout did not hear the words passed between the car's driver and his stepsister, only what the man called to him as he drove away; poor old Herbert Clement heard almost nothing anymore. Odd because my memories of that time, the summer of '79, are awash in music.

My family had spent the previous school year in East Haven, Connecticut. My parents usually taught English at the University of Tennessee at Martin, but my dad swung a teaching exchange with a former colleague at the small Connecticut college where my parents had met and married in the late '60s. The nine months in East Haven were exciting— we lived in a beach house that backed up to the Sound, next door to a seasonal ice cream stand and a year-round needle park. My mother had never liked Tennessee and campaigned my father to find a way to stay in Connecticut, but I was secretly happy to re-enter Martin's atmosphere that May. My parents' home was on a huge block that had as its four corners the elementary school, the school's playground, the municipal pool, and the little league ballpark— a young boy's dreamscape.

Our green, one-story house sat on the corner that was the baseball diamond's home plate, so we were always weeding foul balls from my mother's flowerbeds. I remember the Sun Drop soda machine behind the bleachers there, how hot its metal got by midday and how we begged my father for coins to feed it. I passed all my summer nights across the street at the ball field— I'd gotten back to town in time to play the last few games with my pee-wee team, the undefeated league champions. My first real job was to shag foul balls on the nights my team wasn't playing, for which I was paid in leftover hot dogs, popcorn, and soda at the end of the night. My second job, once I'd grown too old to play little league, was as the league's official scorekeeper and public address announcer, for which I earned seven dollars a game.

I spent the scorching afternoons 200 yards up Clearwater Street from my parents' driveway in the warm waters of the city pool, where my family always bought a summer pass. I remember hearing the Doobie Brothers' "What A Fool Believes" over and over that summer on the little black transistor the lifeguards carried with them up into the deep-end chair. "He came from somewhere back in her long ago." That made me ache inside, though I did not yet have a long ago. Some days Steve Stanford and the high-school guys let me begin a game of "Bombay" with a can opener off the high board. It seemed worth getting sent home to hear Stanford call me "little man," or to hear the pretty lifeguard Lori say as she escorted me out, "don't grow up so soon." During her breaks, Lori relaxed in the shallow end with her boyfriend Randy Finney, whose gleaming gold Honda rested on its kickstand in the pool's parking lot every afternoon. I watched them, her arms around his neck, wondering what went on beneath the water where their legs pretzeled.

The city had built Clearwater Street doubly wide so parents could nose their cars into the spaces painted along that third base line, which made it the perfect place for the high-school band to practice for parade season during the last weeks of August. They practically marched up our driveway, their director walking backwards in front of the flutes, gesticulating wildly and barking orders, stopping them just before someone crashed into my father's garbage cans. In the summer of 1979 they were learning to play Chuck Mangione's "Feels So Good," and I loved to ride my banana-seated blue Schwinn in and out of their ranks, feeling their music fill my body.

I ran across a black and white photograph of myself (see page 106) from that time in a local archive not long ago, the Federal Land Bank t-ball team picture that ran in the *Weakley County Press* in the summer of 1978. I don't know that I'd ever seen it before. I'm kneeling in the lower right corner, screaming "cheese" at the photographer, my new front teeth figuring prominently (the rest of me didn't catch up to those teeth until some time in high school) and my brown locks peeking messily from underneath my baseball cap. On my left hand is the fielder's glove I've had wedged between my mattress and box spring for weeks in anticipation of this first game.

What gets me is my smile. It's positively prelapsarian. Not a goofy smile like the one on the face of Tony Beasley, who stands in the row behind me in the picture, his head cocked hard left, wearing dark-rimmed spectacles and a cap

25

so stiff it looks like he's just taken it from the box. No, my smile bespeaks a joy complete and entire, wholly unself-conscious, the product of a brimming heart as yet unbroken by anything. I feel assured of my parents' love and the safety of my home and summers of swimming and baseball until the end of time. You can see that on my face. I know now none of that assurance was real. Bad things happened to me. Plenty. I've authored my share of misdeeds, too. When I am tempted to think of my childhood as indeed Edenic, I need not look further than Cary's abduction to see I am fooling myself. But the boy in the photo has no idea about any of that, cannot even imagine.

*

Early on the Saturday afternoon of September 1, 1979, Robert Glen Coe's young wife, Tammy, had tried to reach her husband at Carroll County Collision in McKenzie, a body shop where Coe had worked banging out dents the past several months. Coe made it in to work around seven that Saturday morning, the usual time, yet when Tammy Coe called around 12:30 p.m. she was told he'd gone with a co-worker named Chuck to pick up some parts. In the confession he later recanted, Coe claims he drove Chuck's old pickup over to Paris, Tennessee, looking for someone to flash, having all day battled the urge to expose himself, something for which police had picked him up several times before.

Tammy wanted her husband's permission to take their eight-month-old daughter Tammy Rebecca back to Dresden with her sister Vickie, who'd driven her infant son Donnie Lynn the sixteen miles from her home in Dresden to the

Coe's trailer at the Parker Trailer Park in McKenzie for a visit earlier that morning. Tammy also wanted money to buy diapers for the baby they called Rebecca.

Tammy Coe finally reached her husband when she called back a little before 2 p.m., and Vickie drove her and the children to the body shop so Tammy could ask for the diaper money in person. But Coe told her he had none, no cash. Parker Trailer Park proprietor Fred Parker told reporters Coe often complained that the $45 per week he was paying to rent the trailer and the more than twenty additional dollars he spent on diapers and infant formula were breaking him.

Vickie drove Tammy and the children to the Ben Franklin in the McKenzie Shopping Center anyway, where Tammy Coe purchased diapers with money she'd borrowed from her sister, then back to the Coes' trailer for the better part of the afternoon.

The two families often socialized, at least every other weekend, playing penny ante poker and Rook and smoking pot. At one time all four, the sisters and Robert Coe and Vickie's husband Donald Box, had worked at the Kellwood plant in Greenfield making women's coats. The sisters had operated sewing machines and the husbands heavier equipment, but Coe had since moved on to the body shop and Vickie Box had sworn off work and drugs to stay home with the baby. Only her husband, Donald Box, still worked at Kellwood.

Robert Glen Coe came home from work around 3 p.m. that Saturday, changed into blue jeans and a blue shirt, mesh with the number fifty screened on it, then left again, telling Vickie Box he was headed to the home of Jack Lynch, a purported drug contact. Witnesses at his 1981 trial said he spent the night before Cary's disappearance dropping acid, and Coe himself claimed to have been high on pills and pot that night and all the following day, though Vickie Box does not remember that he seemed so. Tammy only said he seemed a little like he was coming down, crashing. No one saw him again until after eight p.m. that evening.

*

Concerned that Cary and Michael had not come home for supper, Mickey Stout went in search of the children around 6:30 and promptly found Michael and both bicycles two and a half blocks away in the parking lot of the Primitive Baptist Church, well beyond where the children were allowed to ride. He raced home to tell Charlotte someone had taken Cary Ann, and the girl's mother, seated at the dinner table eating and not yet dressed for work, threw on some clothes and jumped in her sister's car, the two women scouring the neighborhood for the little girl. Mickey Stout stayed behind and phoned police.

Cary Ann's father, Jerry Medlin, an avionics technician at Memphis Aero, had spent all day visiting his father, a cancer patient at the V.A. Hospital in midtown Memphis, while the old man received chemo treatments. He had planned that Cary Ann would live with him and his new wife Sondra that summer, spend what time was left with her grandfather, but the girl had chosen her new home and her new bike and her brother instead, not that he much blamed her. Jerry and Charlotte had enjoyed a mostly amicable split—"I married him when I was sixteen, we were practically 'arranged,'" says Charlotte Stout, who was raised by her very Pentecostal grandparents on a farm outside Camden, Tennessee. Cary

Ann often asked her mother why they couldn't all just live together, Jerry and his new wife and Charlotte and her new husband.

Charlotte Stout had phoned Jerry early on to let him know that she and Mickey could not find Cary. But when Charlotte called back at 10:00 p.m. in a full-blown panic, the tiny town dark and the girl still missing, Jerry Medlin told Sondra to pack their Traveler mobile home and the two headed the 130 miles north to Charlotte and Mickey's house, leaving a note on the senior Mr. Medlin's door insisting that he not be apprised of his favorite granddaughter's disappearance (he died only days later). It was just going so fast, Charlotte Stout remembers, everything going so fast, people in and out of the house. And somewhere out there everything terrible in the world happening to that little child.

Jerry and Sondra arrived in Greenfield between one and two in the morning and parked the camper adjacent to the Stout home, spending the rest of the night there, though Jerry Medlin did not sleep. His next-door neighbor on Haney Street in Memphis was a local television personality named Mike Lawhead, so Medlin phoned and asked Lawhead if he and his colleagues at Channel 3 might air a spot about the disappearance. The rest of the night and into the morning Medlin walked Greenfield's streets and prayed.

*

Donald Box was at his brother's house tinkering with a truck just before five that evening when he got a call that his wife and sister-in-law and their children had been involved in a minor two-car accident between Greenfield and McKenzie— a man in a pick-up had smashed the fender and bumper of young Mrs. Box's car though no one was hurt. Donald Box had spent the afternoon at his brother's with the idea that the two would go dove hunting, something of a Labor Day weekend tradition ("We supposed to went dove hunting, but it rained," he would later testify). The brothers had decided to fix the truck's flat tire instead and then got to tinkering under the hood.

Donald arrived at the accident scene shortly after getting the call, to assess damage and pick up his wife and sister-in-law and the babies. Donald waited there thirty minutes or so before the five all rode in his car to his father's house and then to Box's own home in Dresden, where they arrived shortly before eight in the evening. Robert Glen Coe joined the others at the Box home in Dresden a little later, explaining that a bridge was out on his usual route between Jack Lynch's home and Dresden and that his alternate route had taken him through the little town of Greenfield. Coe seemed nervous, a little depressed, staring at the floor while the others watched television. Usually he was a cutup, a jokester, calling Kings cowboys when they played cards and such, but Donald Box thought Robert seemed to him to be in a hurry, like he was running from something.

Coe asked Vickie for a muscle relaxer to ease his stomach pain, then he and Donald decided to drive to a Dresden pizza joint called Ben's to pick up dinner. Robert suggested the two men take his car, a gray '72 Ford Gran Torino, two-tone with a brown canvas top, since it was parked behind Donald's. At first the engine wouldn't crank. "I'd be better off dead," Coe told Donnie there in the car.

Once at the pizza parlor, Donnie got change so the brothers-in-law could play pinball while they waited for the pizza. He watched carefully as a deputy sheriff took a seat across the parlor. Robert Glen Coe never looked directly at the deputy. "I want to hurry up and get out of here," Robert told Donald. "I'm hungry." But Robert had little appetite once they got the pizza home. "Robert didn't eat but a piece and a half," Box said later, "and that's not like Robert. Usually when we was around Robert he was always eating, or either he was a big eater."

The two couples watched television and played cards late into the night, Coe becoming more and more relaxed as time wore on. "He got to be his old self," says Donald Box. Box and his wife finally climbed into bed around midnight, Coe and his wife having decided to stay the night there in Dresden, sacking out on the Box's couch. They all slept the night through, peacefully so far as Donald Box can recall.

*

Tennessee Bureau of Investigation Special Agent Alvin Daniel received a call regarding the Medlin case at his home in Troy, Tennessee, at 9 p.m. on the night of the disappearance, a request for assistance from Marlind Gallimore and the Weakley County Sheriff's Department. Alvin Floyd Daniel had begun his law enforcement career as an Air Force M.P. in 1963 before taking a job with the Tennessee Highway Patrol. In 1974, Daniel was promoted to the TBI and had since that time been assigned to the Northwest Tennessee counties of Obion, Weakley, and Lake. Because the Medlin case fell within his jurisdiction, he was chief agent, the man in charge of the case file. Still, Daniel called his supervisor, Inspector Thomas J. "Jack" Blackwell down in Somerville, Tennessee, near Memphis, apprising Blackwell of the apparent kidnapping and requesting additional agents be dispatched to the scene. Daniel then drove the forty or so miles from his home to Mickey Stout's house in Greenfield.

Agent Daniel arrived at the Stout home on Belair around a quarter to ten that night and took a seat at the kitchen table to get descriptions of the little girl— red Harley Davidson t-shirt, red shorts— and of the suspect, which he broadcast on Tennessee Highway Patrol and local sheriff's department frequencies. The girl's parents, he recalls, were frantic. He called Blackwell back to confirm the kidnapping and again requested additional agents, then he called the phone company and requested a tracer be placed on all connected relatives' telephone lines in case a ransom call came in. He placed a recorder on Mickey Stout's home phone, too. Once Blackwell and the five other agents arrived a little after 11 p.m., Agent Daniel led them through a recon of the entire area, then the TBI detail retreated to the Greenfield City Hall building to wait things out.

But as soon as Agent Daniel had driven him past Mickey Stout's modest home, special agent Jack Blackwell knew the little girl was dead. Veteran of twenty years as a peace officer with more than 300 such local law enforcement "assists" and thirty or forty major cases of his own under his belt, he'd been the chief of police in a rural west Tennessee town just like this one before joining the Bureau. "They didn't have a lot," he told a *Jackson Sun* reporter in the weeks leading up to Robert Glen Coe's execution. "I couldn't see kidnapping or ransom when I looked at the house. I said, 'this is not a kidnapping, this is an abduction.' I told Agent Daniel not to tell the family, but this little girl is dead."

Chapter 2:
Search Party

...I slid uncertain feet ahead
behind my flashlight's beam.
Stones, thick roots as twisted as
a ruined body,
what did I fear?
I hoped my batteries
had eight more lives
than the lost child.
I feared I'd find something.

William Matthews, "The Search Party"

Alvin Daniel brought Maggie Lee Stout and her grandson Michael downtown in the early morning hours of Sunday, September 2nd, to assist in the preparation of a composite drawing of the suspect, to be distributed, along with photographs of Cary, to local law enforcement agencies and news media. A detective brought an Idento Kit up from Jackson and sat down with Maggie and Michael and Agent Daniel in the Greenfield City Hall to create the sketch. The man in the composite drawings, it must be said here, while he does bear some resemblance to photos of Robert Glen Coe taken at the time of his arrest days later at the Huntingdon, Tennessee, police station— smallish, beady eyes, a heavy wedge of hair swept across his forehead— seems not to be the man Maggie Stout would describe in her sworn trial testimony in the early spring of 1981, the ugly man with greasy, neck-length hair. (In two separate police lineups later that week, neither Maggie Stout nor her grandson could identify Robert Glen Coe as the stranger in the car.)

Jerry Medlin's neighbor Mike Lawhead and a camera crew from Channel 3 in Memphis arrived at the Stout home around eight that morning and Charlotte Stout and Jerry Medlin taped an appeal for any information regarding their daughter's whereabouts, to be aired later that evening. "We'll do anything you want," the Stouts told the camera. At dawn, Agent Daniel and his crew had begun a routine, house-to-house canvass of the neighborhood surrounding Cary Medlin's home, which lasted through lunchtime. But because it was a holiday weekend, the last holiday of the summer, few families were home. Everybody was at Land Between the Lakes in Kentucky, Daniel surmised, or at Reelfoot Lake. No one had seen anything.

Daniel then enlisted the help of the Weakley County Rescue Squad, comprised of law enforcement officers and lay volunteers from all over the county, assembling the men at noontime inside the huge garage at the Greenfield Fire Station (Daniel had the fire engines backed out to the street) and briefing them on the basic principles of a search. Blackwell and Daniel offered the searchers a description of Cary Medlin and of her abductor and his car. The agents divided the tiny town of Greenfield into quadrants, leaving for themselves the northeast section of town where the girl was last seen and assigning the other areas to Greenfield Police, the county sheriff and his deputies and to the rescue squad chief and his men respectively, conceding that these teams knew the area better than the TBI did. By that time, Daniel, like Blackwell, had accepted that he was looking not for a girl but for a body. "Search ditches, thickets, culverts, hell, Dempsey Dumpsters," Blackwell told the searchers. "If you find anything, clothing or anything, leave it alone. Just holler, let somebody know, but don't touch it."

*

Donald Box says when he woke before 9 a.m. on Sunday morning, September 2nd, Robert and Tammy Coe and little Rebecca were already up and headed out the front door. Coe drove his family directly back to McKenzie, past their own trailer on old Route 4 to the community of Big Buck and the home of his buddy Darrell Ross, whom he'd met when he'd picked Ross up hitchhiking that same stretch of road a few months before. Twenty-one-year-old Ross worked as a custodian at the Carroll County Civic Center to support his sixteen-year-old wife Janet (married to Ross at fourteen) and their daughter, Brandy Joe, fifteen months.

Janet recalls the Coe family pulling into her drive in the Gran Torino a little after nine that morning looking for Darrell. She told Robert her husband was over at his daddy's trying to get their 1971 LeMans running (he'd grown tired of hitching) and Coe pulled away. When he caught up with them later, Janet Ross thought Coe seemed genuinely scared. He told Darrell and Janet a wild story about some trouble with the law, how he and a cousin had been stopped by a state trooper over in Camden with several bags of pot and several buckets of acid in the car and so had shot one trooper and stabbed another in the throat and now needed to skip town. As a strange car approached the Ross home, Janet recalls Coe ran behind the house. "He hollered out to see if everything was clear," she testified, "then we said 'yes' and we all went inside and sit around the stereo and talked."

Alvin Daniel was circling tiny Greenfield in a helicopter around 2 p.m. that Sunday afternoon, September 2nd, when the call came in over the police scanner that rescue workers might have something. They'd hardly been searching an hour. "Unattended" is the word used. No specific reference to a body so as not to excite media or family and draw a crowd. But Jerry Medlin had kept an ear to the police scanner and he made his way from his camper down to City Hall as fast as he could.

Inspector Blackwell had parked near the ball field on Evergreen Street Extended north of town to coordinate search efforts. It was a country ball field, no fences, a good place to land a chopper. He was summoned shortly after two to meet a rescue unit farther out Evergreen toward an unpaved lovers' lane known as Bean Switch Road, where Sheriff's Deputy Charles Gallimore and a rescue squad newcomer named Danny Scott said they had the little girl's body. From their pickup, the two men had noticed some trampled ragweed across a ditch. "It didn't look right," Gallimore told Blackwell. "I said to the boy, 'That don't look right.'"

The men climbed out of the truck and walked about thirty yards before coming upon the corpse. Danny Scott ran back toward the truck screaming and Gallimore yelled after him not to blab everything on the radio. Danny Scott radioed the sheriff to meet the men at their last documented position, where the abandoned access road met Bean Switch. Then he leaned his back against the pickup. A picture of the two men ran in the *Dresden Enterprise* a few days later, Scott wiping his brow, clearly shaken.

The body was so tiny, Charles Gallimore walked closer to make sure it wasn't a little doll. Fifty inches tall and 51 pounds. Gallimore had feared Danny Scott was too green for such heavy work, but the boy was local and knew the roads. Even Gallimore, who would retire with 26 years of service in the sheriff's department, who'd once cut his own aunt out of the mangled wreckage of her car after a head-on collision, had never seen anything so terrible. He never again drove down Bean Switch Road. "Never wanted to," he would later tell a reporter. It proved to be Danny Scott's first and last day with the rescue squad. By the time of the Coe execution twenty years later, when recounting the events of September 2nd Gallimore could not for the life of him remember Danny Scott's name. "The boy," he'd taken to calling him.

Blackwell followed Gallimore 300 yards down a fenced field access road bordered on both sides by soybeans. The roadbed itself was overgrown, weeds and saplings shoulder-high, some as tall as Blackwell himself. There had been a homeplace at the end of the road at one time, and a barn, but there was nothing now, only a crude boat slip at the creek for coon hunters and their dogs. When I came to see the place 25 years later, in a car I'd rented at the Nashville airport, I startled a man just about to put his boat into the creek there (startled myself too, considering what I'd come to see) and backed that car all the way to the main road as fast as I dared.

The men came to a gap in the brush line, an old gate. The mouth of another abandoned road. And finally, from there, Inspector Jack Blackwell could see Cary Ann Medlin's body lying on its back 85 feet down in the weed patch. She looked to be sleeping but with eyes wide open, flies swarming the dried blood on her cheek and neck where the greasy-haired stranger had stabbed her. Her red shorts were rumpled only slightly at the crotch so that you could see a thin white strip of her panties. She was barefoot, as usual, her white sandals lying a few feet from the body, arranged neatly side-by-side.

"Don't you touch a thing," Blackwell yelled to Gallimore, who was still standing over Cary Ann. "Get an ambulance back in here," he called ahead to Danny Scott, who roused himself and wiped his mouth and climbed into the truck's cab to make the call.

*

I saw those crime scene photos, in a courthouse law library in Jackson, Tennessee, sealed inside a manila folder at the bottom of a tattered cardboard file box. I'd come home to visit the crime scene and Cary's grave and to read transcripts of Coe's original 1981 Memphis murder trial. The courthouse clerks were pleasant but seemed surprised at my interest; they all knew the story and that most everyone involved was now dead— Coe and his little victim, even Agents Blackwell and Daniel. The lead prosecutor was upstairs in that very courthouse, they told me, now a criminal court of appeals judge.

I found many references to the photos as "exhibits" in the transcript so that when I came upon the envelope I figured I knew what was inside. I felt eerily like part of that original search party, most afraid that I'd actually find something. At first I couldn't look and got up to take a lunch break, walking all the way to my car out in the parking lot before I turned around and went back inside. But I did come back: if I was going to do this thing, I had to be willing to look at the worst of it.

I laid the envelope in front of myself on the desk in the small library cubicle and opened its brads, then slid the large prints from inside and laid them before me on the table. The girl in the pictures looked almost exactly as I'd remembered her, yet unmistakably dead, splayed awkwardly in the weeds. John Everett Millais's drowned Ophelia, only bone-dry. I thought of the last time I'd seen her, through the chain link fence of the University Courts swimming pool. "What are you doing here?" she'd called out. It was a good question, then and now.

I went to lunch and ordered a plate of food but couldn't eat a bite. I drove the rental car the fifty miles to my parents' house where I was spending the night and brought the photocopies I'd made inside with me. Only my mother would look, still determined, I think, to protect me.

*

Reporters and other onlookers had already swarmed the mouth of the abandoned roadbed by the time Jerry Medlin arrived to identify his daughter. They'd been shooed away once already to make way for the white ambulance, which was swallowed by the road, scraping low-hanging branches all the way down to where Blackwell and the others waited. The driver had it idling down by the old gate. Now the crowd would have to be dispersed again for the next of kin.

Jerry Medlin had run smack into a harried Alvin Daniel at City Hall and insisted on being taken immediately to the scene, against Agent Daniel's better judgment and advice. Too shaken to drive, Medlin rode in the passenger seat of his father-in-law's car as Daniel led the two men to Bean Switch Road. Once at the murder scene, Jerry Medlin climbed right inside the ambulance and saw it was his little girl.

Medlin was to be the only family member to see the corpse that day. Maggie Lee Stout insisted her boy Mickey not be allowed to view his stepdaughter's body— Mickey began to tremble even as investigators escorted him toward the ambulance, saying he needed his medicine. Both he and the girl's mother were under sedation in the hours and days following the discovery. ("It isn't helping much," investigators told reporters.)

Charlotte Stout had "sort of come apart," Jerry Medlin told the court at Robert Glen Coe's trial, crying and screaming when she heard the news. Her doctor, Martin physician O.K. Smith, was on hand in case the stress and trauma brought on pre-term labor. Mickey Stout had been the one to break it to her. "They found her," he told his wife. "Baby, she's dead."

Many years later, Jerry Medlin would get "saved" and become an ordained Baptist preacher near his new home in Florida. In testimonials about his old life, he often describes the events of that terrible Sunday in a sermon he calls "Precious Memories." As the others came apart around him, a whole house of wailing men and women, Jerry Medlin remembers walking off as he'd done the night before, this time toward the sunny edge of the woods near the murder scene, not so much praying now as asking God how he could take an eight-year-old girl. "What kind of a God are you?" he said aloud. Then Medlin says for the first time God spoke to him in the "still, small voice" he'd heard about all his church-going life. "If you had been doing right this past six years," God told him, "maybe I wouldn't have let this happen. I done this to break your craggy old heart and make it new."

Chapter 3:
Manhunt

Greenfields are gone now, parched by the sun... Gone with the cold wind that swept into my heart... Where are the greenfields that we used to roam?

The Brothers Four, "Greenfields"

The white ambulance brought Cary Ann Medlin's body out to Bean Switch Road late that Sunday afternoon, then east to Highway 45 and on to Interstate 40 toward Memphis, practically retracing the route her father had taken in his camper the night before, only in the opposite direction this time and wholly without hope or urgency.

Agent Robert Yoakum followed along to take photographs of the girl's clothes and impressions of her bare footprint. Memphis Pathologist James Spencer Bell found, in addition to the solitary stab wound visible on Cary Ann's neck at the scene, small hemorrhages of the skin on the little girl's face, suggesting the killer had also tried to strangle her, concluding that the stabbing and manual strangulation combined caused the girl's death and that the whole awful business probably took six or seven minutes.

There was so little blood at the scene, officers had doubted the girl had been killed on Bean Switch Road, assuming the body had been dumped there later. But Dr. Bell's single stab wound/strangulation theory suggested a Bean Switch Road murder was indeed possible, and though Weakley County

Sheriff Marlind Gallimore initially reported that authorities did not suspect the girl had been sexually molested, Bell found bruising consistent with sexual assault, "live" lesions suggesting Cary Ann had been violated prior to her death. Elizabeth Fowler, a forensic serologist, found semen and spermatozoa on the swabs provided her by Dr. Bell.

*

Maggie Lee and Joe William Stout and their grandson had traveled to the Weakley County Jail in Dresden Sunday afternoon so Maggie and Michael could view suspects in a police lineup.

"Remember yesterday?" Joe Stout asked his grandson once inside the jailhouse. "I want you to look in there and see if you see him."

"Okay. What if he's not in there?' Michael asked. Nashville *Tennessean* reporters suggested the elfin boy had little grasp of the tragedy.

"That's alright," his grandfather told him.

"This is going to be harder than I thought," said the boy before going in.

The grisly story was front-page news in papers statewide— the *Tennessean*, *The Jackson Sun*, and Memphis *Commercial Appeal*. The Tuesday, September 4th edition of the Martin bi-weekly, the *Weakley County Press*, reported that at press time no suspects were being held in connection to the crime and that Governor Lamar Alexander and a host of local politicians had offered a $5,000 reward to anyone furnishing information leading to the arrest and conviction of Cary Ann Medlin's murderer.

Two men had been picked up in the area-wide manhunt

in recent days but none were charged with the crime. One, eighteen-year-old J.D. Azbill, a neighbor and acquaintance of Robert Glen Coe's at the Parker Trailer Court, had been arrested during a church service in McKenzie and was being held on charges he'd raped another little girl, six years old, whom he'd agreed to babysit, but Azbill had been ruled out as a suspect in the Medlin slaying.

The other suspect, a Greenfield man named Donald Gant, had been picked up for questioning but subsequently released for what authorities considered a lack of evidence. Gant, whom Sheriff Marlind Gallimore said so strongly resembled the man in the composite drawing that the sketch "could have been a photograph" (Maggie and Michael Stout both identified Gant in the lineup), had been arrested early on Monday the 3rd in the Gibson County town of Milan, between Greenfield and Jackson, with fresh bloody scratches on his neck and no solid alibi for the night of Cary Medlin's abduction, changing his story many times before finally admitting he had in fact been in Greenfield the night of the murder. Gant had a history of inappropriate sexual advances toward young girls and investigators found bloody clothing and bedding in his home. But Gant had no brown car nor access to one and when he did not crack under questioning, authorities released him.

*

I learned Cary was dead that Sunday evening. My mother was in our driveway talking to another mother who had stopped to pick up or drop off a playmate. It was after supper and all four of my parents' children— I'm the second child, the elder of two sons— were outside in the twilight.

We usually spent hours outside after supper, riding bikes in the driveway or catching lightning bugs or playing tag or whiffle ball.

My mother called me over to the woman's idling car. Hadn't I known this girl? Yes, I said, she had been in my class. Mom was sure she'd also been in my younger sister Ruth's dance class, taught by a young German named Cornelia, the wife of a language professor my mom said was too young to be so severe.

My mother says I didn't badger her with questions, nor did she and my father dwell on the matter. What should a child be told about such a thing? Coe did not become a bogeyman, subject of ghost stories or kid's games. In the days following, we were made to understand Cary's murder as a thing that happened, albeit terrible, and that she was in God's house now.

I do remember somehow coming to understand that the murder weapon had been an ice pick (that was the rumor immediately after the crime) and since my school teacher's son had fallen on an ice pick and spent several days in the hospital that year, and since as a boy I'd always eaten ice cubes from freezer trays, for many years I associated ice picks only with danger.

A few years ago, a drunken student from the small New York college where I teach drowned in the river that flows through the town and past our home. Rows of volunteers, students and townspeople, paraded silently through the backyards in our neighborhood that November week, checking sheds and basements and garages for the body. Divers found him days later in the cold river just below my wife's hair salon while I was out of town on business. "I guess your student's dead," my son Jackson, then four, said to me matter-of-factly upon my return. I chided my wife at first for telling the boy, but I see now there was no keeping it from him. Of course he'd seen it all, police tape and the solemn rows of searchers. I watched him closely to see if I might remember how I'd felt all those years ago, with no real luck. For a while after, he seemed afraid of the river and sometimes even now when we cross it on the Main Street bridge he'll mention the kid. "That's where your student died," he'll say from the backseat.

My old grade school friend David Nanney is fond of saying that growing up in Martin was like growing up in Andy Griffith's Mayberry— he moved to Memphis before high school and so has a particularly rosy view of our lives in Weakley County. David says that before the murder, his mother let him and his brother Doug play among the headstones at the East Side Cemetery near their home from dinner until sundown. My brother and sisters and I similarly had the run of our giant block: the playgrounds, the pool, the baseball and softball diamonds. I remember vividly the ends of those summers, after baseball season but before school had begun again, how lonesome our once-busy block seemed. Hardly a car passed, except the city exterminator's pick-up circling once a month or so, spraying for mosquitoes. 'Do Not Follow' said a sign in the cab's rear window, but we climbed on our bikes to catch up, inhaling that strange fog.

Things changed some after the murder: Mrs. Nanney kept closer tabs, David says, my mother, too. An item of the front page of the *Weakley County Press* two weeks after the murder, titled "Learn to Live," proclaimed that life in Weakley County would "never be the same," that "the ever-changing society of today has dealt us a bad blow." "On a daily basis we experience crimes through the news medias [sic]," explained the *Press* writer, "but living in a rural area we are almost isolated from the cruel outside world." Only when a death like Cary's happens in our own backyard, "when our Utopian life is shattered," wrote the reporter, do we really appreciate life." A similar editorial ran in *The Jackson Sun* with the headline "Tragedy Serves As Grim Reminder For Area Parents." What happened to Cary was an example of what could happen "to any child," wrote *Sun* reporter Gail Boyd, "at any time."

*

Robert and Tammy Coe and their daughter spent Sunday night at Darrell Ross's home in Big Buck. Labor Day morning, both young families headed to the home of Darrell Ross's father for coffee, where Janet Ross says Robert Glen Coe asked Ross, Sr. if he had a pistol to sell, but the man had none. Coe then asked Janet Ross to dye his hair so folks wouldn't recognize him. He wanted to perm his hair as well, but neither Ross nor Tammy Coe knew how to set a perm. The families piled back into the Torino and drove to Ben Franklin in McKenzie to buy hair dye, Miss Clairol Velvet Blue Black, and Janet applied it to Robert's hair. "It was dark," Janet Ross told the Memphis court at Coe's trial. "Real dark, but it looked natural," she said, impressed with her handiwork.

The following morning, Tuesday, September 4th, Coe and Darrell Ross left the Ross home at eight a.m. driving Coe's Torino, but Janet told the court they returned more than three hours later in a blue Ford Mustang, "Mach Two" stenciled in silver on its side. Barry Jones, owner of Crestview Motors in Gleason, the town which lies between McKenzie and Dresden along Highway 22, testified at the Coe trial that he'd originally sold the '72 Torino to Coe and his mother, Annabelle, in June of '79 but that Coe had returned to trade the car for the Mustang early that September Tuesday. Jones and his wife, Aletha, Crestview's bookkeeper, remembered Coe as having dirty blonde hair earlier that summer, but at the time of the trade-in noted he'd dyed his hair jet black. The couple remembered seeing dark, thumb-sized smudges of hair dye on Coe's forehead near the hairline.

Robert Glen Coe was still antsy that Tuesday morning and planned to leave town as soon as he could, that evening if possible. Tammy Coe had gone back to her sewing machine at a pajama factory in McKenzie that morning, but left at lunchtime to get some pictures developed, pictures she and Janet had made of their children, then rode with her husband and the Ross family out to where Robert's boss lived to see if Coe might pick up his check early.

After Tammy Coe returned to work, Darrell and Janet Ross and baby Brandy took Robert Glen Coe to the bus station ten miles east in Huntingdon to see about a Greyhound ticket. Coe didn't purchase a ticket at that time but did when the families returned to the station early that evening, after Tammy Coe came home from work, where she'd given her two weeks notice. She and her husband had hatched a plan: Robert Glen Coe would travel by bus to Marietta, Georgia, that evening, maybe push farther in a few days, back to Florida where he'd moved with his mother several years ago after dropping out of the seventh grade at Gleason Junior High. Once he'd established himself, gotten a job and a place to live, he'd send for Tammy and the baby. Darrell Ross and Janet and Brandy planned on coming, too, eventually. Tammy had an uncle all the way down in Tampa who'd promised to set them all up with jobs and new digs.

But time was running short for Coe. His own sister Bonnie, following the events on television, had called the Sheriff's Office in Obion County where she lived and given deputies her brother's name as someone who matched the physical description and had a troubled history with police (she said years later she'd called in thinking Coe might get some help while in custody).

Acting on the Obion County tip, broadcast on area law enforcement frequencies, the Gleason Police Chief asked Aletha Jones of Crestview Motors about cars traded in that day, and she led him to the '72 Torino. She described Robert Coe and Darrell Ross and the strange circumstances of the trade-in that morning. TBI investigators arrived shortly thereafter— they'd gone to Coe's trailer first and now had Darrell and Janet Ross cuffed in the backseat— and asked her to move the car to a garage on site where they dusted the car's interior for prints (evidence never mentioned at the Coe trial) and took impressions of the tire treads. Investigators asked Mrs. Jones to let no one other than law enforcement officials near the automobile.

Alvin Daniel then called Greenfield and had Maggie and Michael Stout driven out to identify the car as the one they'd seen rolling slowly on Fairlane Drive three days earlier, the one into which Michael had seen his stepsister climb. While at Crestview, Agent Daniel heard on the scanner that Coe had been stopped by Huntingdon Police while trying to board a Trailways bus for Georgia. He and Blackwell covered the twenty miles between Gleason and McKenzie "at emergency speed."

Coe had booked a ticket to Marietta under the pseudonym "James Watson" and the address on his luggage was that of his brother, Roger Coe. Huntingdon police arrested him without a struggle and with three bags of marijuana in his possession. Huntingdon officers said they first thought he'd colored his hair with shoe polish, it looked so bad.

At 5:45 p.m., Agents Daniel and Blackwell rendezvoused with local police at the Huntingdon Police Station, where Coe and his cohorts had been brought for questioning. Daniel noted a man he took to be Coe standing with a police officer at the dispatcher's desk. Coe was being booked on the marijuana possession charge, the agents learned from a state trooper also in the station, so the agents waited their turn and then approached Coe and offered their credentials. Coe had been released from custody at this point and was for all intents and purposes free to go, but he agreed to a word with Daniel and Blackwell. The Huntingdon dispatcher led the three men to a small room "right off to the side of the dispatcher's office," Daniel recalls, where he and Blackwell planned a preliminary interrogation of their suspect.

Coe waived his Miranda rights at 5:55 p.m. that Tuesday evening, ten minutes after the TBI had arrived. He initially denied involvement in or knowledge of the case, claiming to have spent the night in Dresden at the Box home. When Daniel asked about the dyed hair and the assumed name, Coe said he'd told his friends the story about the state trooper over in Camden and had to follow through on the ruse. Coe seemed to Daniel to be sober and rational and a search of his person turned up no needle marks or fingernail scratches, only what appeared to be fecal material on the end of his penis, under the foreskin. Coe said it was indeed "shit," that he'd attempted to have anal sex with his wife earlier that day, unsuccessfully. "Does sex with your wife not satisfy you?" Daniel would later ask him. "No, sir," he told him.

The agents drove Coe back to the Huntingdon bus station to retrieve his luggage and then on to the Weakley County Jail in Dresden for further questioning. Blackwell was thinking of the coroner's report and Cary's injuries and what he and Daniel had found during the strip search. He was certain they had the right man.

"I did it," Coe told the agents, no sooner than they'd seated him in the conference room in Dresden. Perhaps he'd seen his wife Tammy in the jail's outer lobby.

"You did what, Robert?" Daniel asked him.

"I killed that little girl," he said.

Daniel motioned for Blackwell to come into the room, then allowed Tammy Coe to come in also. Coe took his wife in his arms and began to cry.

"I did it," he said again, this time to Tammy, "I killed that little girl." Something else was said between the Coes but agent Daniel was setting up his tape recorder and did not hear.

Chapter 4:
Old Soul

Hey Carrie-Anne, what's your game now, can
anybody play?

The Hollies, "Carrie-Anne"

Charlotte Stout can't quite remember how she and Jerry Medlin arrived at their daughter's name. "There was probably a song going around at that time," she says. Perhaps the Hollies' "Carrie-Ann," a top-ten *Billboard* hit for Graham Nash and his English bandmates in 1967.

Charlotte says she was an ignorant little girl of fourteen when she met sixteen-year-old Jerry at a friend's birthday party that year. She lived what she considered a very sheltered life with her Pentecostal grandparents in the town of Camden in Benton County, just west of the Tennessee River. She had moved with her mother and stepfather to Rancho Cucamonga, California, a few years earlier but wanted to move back to Camden almost immediately, disliking the pace of life out west, the smog, the danger. "Get me back to Tennessee," Charlotte remembers thinking. Her mother's strict parents agreed to take her in.

Once Charlotte turned sixteen, some friends arranged a double date for her and Jerry Medlin, who had grown up Missionary Baptist on a family farm in Henry County, Tennessee, near the town of Bruceton. It was Charlotte's first date, she told me when I called her from my parents' house three years ago. "I think Jerry was attracted to my purity," she says. "I'm a very, very, very Christian person."

Charlotte and Jerry were married in 1968 and Cary Ann was born October 9, 1970 (she shares a birthday with my younger sister Ruth). Their daughter was a joy, her mother says, cheerful and chatty, something which later caused her schoolteachers much consternation but made her a favorite of most other grown-ups. "She would talk and talk and talk," says Charlotte. "Sometimes I'd just have to ask her to stop talking. I'd say, 'Girl, my ears are tired.'"

Cary loved Kool-Aid and spaghetti (which she called "pusghetti") and Pink Panther cartoons, though her mother says she rarely sat still long enough to watch an entire episode. Despite this energy, Charlotte says Cary was rarely in trouble at home, almost never punished, because she so hated to displease.

Charlotte entered the girl in a beauty review the year she turned seven but the judges hadn't even called Cary back for the second round. Mrs. Stout found Cary Ann backstage, crying.

"Do you still love me?" the girl asked her mother.

"Of course I still love you," Charlotte told Cary Ann. "Why would you ask such a thing?"

"Because I didn't win."

Charlotte says she told Cary she was the prettiest one out there, the judges just didn't know it. At a service held for Cary at the Victims of Violence Children's Memorial Garden in Nashville in the days preceding the Robert Glen Coe execution in 2000, Charlotte Stout hung the dress Cary had worn in the pageant from the garden's wooden archway, a white dress adorned with pastel flowers.

Earlier, when Charlotte tried to break four-year-old

Cary of a thumb-sucking habit, resorting even to sprinkling the girl's thumb with ground black pepper, only Charlotte's tearful pleading seemed to make a difference. Cary Ann sucked her peppered thumb until tears welled in her eyes, pulling the thumb out of her mouth only to try to scrape off some of the pepper. "She was frowning at me the whole time," her mother says. Only when an exasperated Charlotte started to cry and say "Please stop!" did the little girl relent.

Charlotte had met Mickey on another double date, this time arranged by the gang at Maggie Lee's. Twenty-three-year-old Charlotte wasn't quite so naïve as she'd been on her first blind date, by then a mother and nursing student at Tennessee-Martin. The marriage seemed a good thing for Cary Ann— she gained a little brother and another doting daddy.

Among children her own age, Charlotte Stout says Cary Ann was always very "mothering." To her new stepbrother Michael, that was just another way of saying "bossy." "She was strong-willed," Michael remembers years later, a grown man and father now. "That's how she was to me— I was her little brother." Once when she and her cousin found a ten-dollar bill on the ground, they disagreed about what to do with the money— the cousin wanted to save it, but Cary insisted they buy a toy soda machine she had seen at Wal-Mart. The cousin eventually conceded to buying that soda fountain. "When she turned those brown eyes on you," her mother says, "you didn't stand a chance."

Sandy Smith remembers Cary as a silly-hearted friend. The girls were the same age and shared the Belair Drive neighborhood. In fact, Cary and Michael had stopped by Sandy's home on the Saturday afternoon of the abduction to see if Sandy wanted to join them, and the *Dresden Enterprise* ran a haunting photo the following Monday of young Sandy keeping vigil for her friend in the shade of a giant oak, her pony tail silhouetted against the setting sun.

Cary Ann's canary yellow bicycle had become her prized possession, her mother says, her calling card around the little town, but after her death it was the first thing she gave away. "I didn't keep a lot of her things," she told reporters years later, "it was too painful." Only the pageant dress and the school photos, a pair of bronzed baby shoes. For a long time Charlotte ordered Cary's bedroom locked and allowed no one inside.

Sometimes even now, Charlotte Stout, mother to two grown boys born after her daughter's murder, tells Mickey she wishes Cary Ann were here so the two could go shopping. "My sons don't want to go shopping with Mommy," Charlotte Stout explains. "I wish I had all my life with my daughter— I look at other mothers and daughters going shopping and doing things and that really makes my heart hurt. I wish I had my whole life with her, but I don't."

Mrs. Stout does take comfort in Robert Glen Coe's account of Cary Ann's final moments, how she bore witness to God's love and died for it. (He told investigators Cary had told him "Jesus loves you" just before he killed her.) "She told Coe what he needed to hear, whether he wanted to hear it or not," her mother says. "She didn't understand lying. Whenever a friend of hers would tell a lie— and she knew they were lying— she couldn't understand why they were doing that. When I heard that she had told Coe, 'Jesus loves you,' I was so relieved. I knew she was okay. I knew Jesus had been there with her, that He'd taken care of her."

That became the consensus among those closest to Cary Ann: that she was a tiny martyr, like the girl at Columbine High School shot because she would not deny her God. Demons came into Greenfield that September afternoon, explains the Stouts' pastor, the Reverend Jerry Lusby of the Greenfield First Baptist Church, and the demons went into Robert Glen Coe, determined to prevent Cary Ann from spreading Christ's message of salvation. But Lusby says the demons were defeated, that Cary Ann lives on in her influence on others.

"In eight years, Cary accomplished more for God and people's hearts than most people do in an old-age lifetime," her father Jerry Medlin told a crowd gathered at Cary's grave in 1999 to protest another stay of the Coe execution. "I couldn't be prouder of that child if she'd lived to be 150 years old. She said a few words to a man who was about to do her harm," Medlin told protesters. "I can't think of a better way to go out than by giving God glory and spreading the good news that He loves you. Her life wasn't all in vain— God got glory from something bad."

"She probably was an eighty-year-old person in an eight-year-old's body, with all the wisdom and knowledge she had," Cary's stepfather Mickey Stout told the crowd. "That's why Charlotte says she was an 'old soul.'"

*

The last time I saw Cary Ann, I was swimming at the pool at the University Courts housing complex on the UTM campus, a small rectangular in-ground pool at the center of the complex, near the community center and laundry room. We Cowser kids were usually at the city pool down the street (with my mother when we were very young— Dad did not swim— and by ourselves as we got older). But this must have been the summer when that pool was closed all season for major repairs, so once or twice we swam at University Courts.

Cary called my name, pleasant surprise in her voice. "Hey Bobby Cowser!"

I squinted to see her in the noonbright sun. Was she still living in an apartment there? She sat astride a bicycle (whether it was the canary yellow number I do not recall), her fingers entwined in the chain link of the pool fence.

"What are you doing here?" she yelled.

This was the summer after our second grade year, just before my family went on our nine-month Connecticut hiatus. We would return to Martin the following May but Cary would have already moved with her family to Greenfield. She was dead by the following September, before I ever saw her again.

It's difficult to say why that moment figures so prominently in memory. Or maybe not difficult at all, easily attributable to the regular operation of memory and the general solipsism of children— she remains the only murder victim I've ever known.

It seems impossibly hard to eulogize a girl not even nine years old, ridiculous even, like trying to compute how old her soul may have been. One of our first-grade classmates remembers that Cary Ann cried easily and often, perhaps when scolded for her chattiness, but I have no memory of that. David Nanney was in that first grade class, too. She always called him by his full name. "Okay, David Nanney," he can hear her saying.

I do have this stubborn idea, though, that Cary and I

shared a bond, as fellow chatterboxes. In memory she does seem genuinely pleased to see me there in the pool. But I may have imagined that, too. James McConkey points to the intimate relationship between imagination and memory, both faculties constructing images from material not currently before us. Imagination and memory are two sides of the same coin, says Vanderbilt writer Tony Earley.

*

A week before her daughter's death, Charlotte says Cary claimed to have heard someone calling her name from the top of the stairs in the family's Belair Drive home.

"Make them quit saying my name," Cary told her mother. She sat at the bottom of the staircase.

"Who?" her mother asked her from the kitchen. "There's nobody up there."

Cary looked at her mother and pointed up the stairs. "They're right there," Cary said.

Charlotte walked over to where Cary was sitting. "Okay," she said, pointing up the stairs. "Look up there. There's nobody there. Do you see anybody?"

"No," Cary said.

"Then who's calling your name?" Charlotte asked her.

"I don't know, but they're right there."

"What are they saying?"

"They're saying Cary, Cary, Cary, over and over again," the girl told her. "They're calling my name." She jumped up and ran out to play.

At the time, Charlotte chalked it up to a fever Cary had been running. The girl's been sick, Charlotte told herself, she's hallucinating. Now, though, she knows little Cary Ann heard the angels calling her home.

Charlotte hardly visits her daughter's grave these days, only every once in a while to change the flowers. "Cary's not there," she explains, "Cary's with God."

Nor does she pray for the little girl because no one can hurt her now. Charlotte says she plans to see her daughter one day, on that far shore. "Oh, I'll see the little chatterbox. I'll say 'Your hair needs combing, girl, get your shoes on.'"

On Thursday, September 6, 1979, Cary Ann Medlin's body was laid to rest in the Highland Cemetery in Greenfield, following a 1 p.m. funeral service at the First Baptist Church, where she'd attended church and Sunday school. Brother John Harrison officiated the ceremony. "It really has been a shock to our town," Harrison's wife told *The Commercial Appeal*, "Children from our church called our house all day Sunday wanting to know if the body had been found."

The body rests there yet, at what is still the back of the cemetery, near a fence beyond which cattle graze and a creek flows lazily. I visited on my way back to my parents' house after a day at the courthouse with the trial transcripts. The headstone bears Cary's name and dates of her short life, that first-grade photo mounted in a cameo frame. Also a quotation from the Arab poet Khalil Gibran, offered by her stepfather, Mickey:

> *When you are sorrowful, look again in your heart,*
> *and you shall see that in truth you are weeping*
> *for that which has been your delight.*

Chapter 5:
Poor White

There's one more kid that'll never go to school,
never get to fall in love, never get to be cool...

Neil Young, "Rockin' in the Free World"

Dinnertime was storytime when we were kids, and we always begged my father to tell the story of the two boys from his tiny east Texas hometown (a town once known as Twin Groceries but since renamed Saltillo) who robbed a local bank while the traveling rodeo was passing through. Billy Rex and Jerry Max Pickett. How we howled at the names. The story went that Dad brought magazines to Billy Rex at the county jail after the young man's arrest, and if the names were the set-up, the punch line was what Billy said to my father, which Dad learned to save until we'd caught our collective breath.

"Bobby," Billy Rex told my father, "they done ree-voked mah pee-roll." We'd explode again.

At first, the names couldn't have been funny to my father, who had known so many like it in Old Saltillo: his cousins Greenberry Griffith and Marvel Wardrup and Welcome Gene Barnett, his Uncle Happy and his Aunt Moley, his grade school sweetheart Ellouine Goswick. He was eventually a good sport about our laughter, though I recall him saying to my mother once as he left the table, "these children don't respect me." I'm afraid he was right. When I was in junior high I respected my handsome young football coach Rick Wilson and practically no one else. My father seemed impossibly old to me, from a remote world dusty and sepia-toned.

My mother's suppertime stories were usually cautionary, easy to interpret. My father's— about the boy who killed a rival at a school dance over a girl's locket, or the gay school teacher run out of town in the night, or this one about the rodeo robbery— were more opaque, gothic. They captivate me now, and I see there was more to the story of the Pickett boys than we could have understood as children.

*

Former Weakley County Sheriff's Deputy Wayne Pendergrass claims to have been the first lawman on the scene that September afternoon off Bean Switch Road in Greenfield. " I still have nightmares about it," he says. He'd been ordered by Sheriff Marlind Gallimore to protect the integrity of the crime scene, literally a patch of weeds, and in the early days of Coe's incarceration, as the accused appeared for arraignment and grand jury hearings, it was Pendergrass who brought Coe to the courthouse in Dresden. "I hauled him back and forth to Fort Pillow [State Prison]," Pendergrass explains. "He delighted in telling me what he done. I advised him of his rights and told him not to talk about it. He said, 'I don't care, I done it.' Like he was proud of it."

Though he was to grow agitated and even surly before judges as his execution approached, most newspaper accounts of Coe's early days in court refer to his flat, emotionless affect. He appeared at his arraignment in the same clothes he'd been arrested in, the blue jeans and football jersey, and told the judge simply, "No," when asked if he could afford an attorney. Still, Mike Wilson, another former sheriff's deputy who later became Weakley County sheriff, says that he knew when he looked into Coe's eyes that he'd seen the face of a killer.

*

Robert Glen Coe was born on April 15, 1956, in Hickman County, Kentucky, in the far southwest corner of the state, to angry, hard-drinking sharecropper Willie Coe and his wife Annabelle. Hickman County had originally been Louisiana Purchase territory and remains the most sparsely populated and among the poorest counties in the commonwealth. Like Carl Perkins, who grew up just below the Kentucky border in an unincorporated town in Lake County, Tennessee, or Johnny Cash, born down on the delta in Arkansas, Coe was born to impoverished folk who worked farms along the little rivers that drained west into the Mississippi, the Obion and the Deer and the Bayou de Chien. Coe's parents moved the family— older sister Bonnie, older brothers Roger and Jimmy (born deaf), Robert and Billie Jean— from farm shack to farm shack throughout rural west Tennessee and western Kentucky, finally settling near Gleason, Tennessee, in eastern Weakley County, where Robert attended school through the seventh grade.

The Coe family often lived without running water or enough to eat, and the stories of abuse at Willie Monroe Coe's hand curdle the blood. The title of this chapter is taken from an early twentieth-century novel by Sherwood Anderson, but one defense attorney actually likened Coe's early life to something out of the work of Georgia writer Erskine Caldwell, whose chronicling of the desperate southern sharecropping experience in novels like *Tobacco Road* and *God's Little Acre* serves as a kind of counterpoint to the "moonlight and magnolias" fare Caldwell found so unrealistic. Poverty drives Caldwell's characters to states of ignorance and selfishness such that they are at the mercy of their basest appetites, and there is every indication the Coe family lived that way, too.

Youngest son Robert got the worst of his father's wrath. His siblings say the beatings began while Robert was still in utero— Coe's father claimed Annabelle had been unfaithful and that the baby wasn't his, beating Robert's mother unmercifully for her transgression. Billie Jean says her father, a heavy-set man, six feet tall and more, would "whop" shrimpy Robert "for no reason." His sisters say their father threw the three year-old little boy against the wall and kicked him off a porch, that Willie threw a claw hammer at five-year-old Robert's head, knocking him unconscious (this head trauma the source, some experts argued later, for much of Robert Glen Coe's psycho-social dysfunction). When at age eight Coe tried to flee one of his father's beatings, Willie Coe pulled out a gun and shot his son in the leg. Psychiatrists who evaluated Robert later report he remembered his father telling him as he lay on the ground, "I hate you, I hate your guts."

Little Robert grew to fear his father so that he would not walk past him to use the bathroom, often waiting until he soiled himself instead. Willie Coe himself spent time in mental institutions in the early 1960s after abuse and incest charges and repeated suicide threats. Once, after Willie Coe had actually placed a gun to his own chest and fired, Coe and his siblings were sure the man was dead, and Robert remembers that as the happiest moment of his life. But the bullet missed Willie Coe's heart and he survived.

If he had poverty and abuse in common with Perkins and Cash, Robert Glen Coe did not share their genius. Coe struggled in school, failing first, second, fifth, sixth, and seventh grades. Many experts believe Coe may have been not only mentally ill (a battery of psychiatrists diagnosed Coe as suffering from everything from bipolar disorder to paranoid schizophrenia and sexual deviation with compulsive features, and he was medicated for the condition all the time he was in prison) but also mentally retarded, though experts aren't sure whether the retardation was congenital or a result of all the early head trauma. (At the bottom level of poverty and despair," James Baldwin writes in *Evidence of Things Not Seen*, "it is difficult to judge who is 'retarded.'")

Kids at school teased him mercilessly, calling him "Crawdad" because he smelled so bad and was so dirty. He had squinty eyes and a devious look about him, some said, and fought back when other children provoked him. Steven Ross, who attended Gleason schools in the late 1960s and is now a Gleason accountant, remembers little Robert Coe as mischievous but not mean. "He was dirty, nasty, and not well-cared for," Ross told *The Jackson Sun*. "You could tell there wasn't a lot of raising going on [in the Coe household]."

Many classmates remember Coe begging for food, and Steven Ross recalls Coe once asking to have two biscuits Ross was carrying on the school bus. "The poor do not awaken to breakfast," James Baldwin writes. "They wake up to whatever there is." For the record, Ross did not share his biscuits. Poverty, says Baldwin, "elicits from the land of opportunity and the work ethic a judgment as merciless as it is defensive."

Ross and his classmates saw no indication in Coe's behavior that he might be capable of the crime for which he was convicted and ultimately executed. The Gleason elementary principal agreed, saying Coe was not unlike the dozens of towheaded boys who passed through the doors of his school each day. "I can't believe how much he changed in ten years," the principal said.

*

I did not know Robert Glen Coe growing up, but I knew many like him. My school friends lived in subdivisions with names like "Scenic Hills" and "Glenwood" and "Oakwood Estates," but our house on Virginia Street, for all its proximity to the pool and the school and the ball fields and for all our idyllic days there, was also one street over from Martin's one truly rough thoroughfare, aptly named Meek Street. Some of my brother's friends ribbed him about living so close, asking him how things were in "Meek's Division."

Robert Glen Coe's cousin Tammy Poore told the court he spent the Friday night before Cary Medlin's murder at her home on Meek Street, dropping acid and smoking weed. That fact made an eerie kind of sense to me when I discovered it in the transcript of the trial; it literally brought things home. Meek Street and my backyard both abutted Highway 22, which carried you out quickly to Maggie Lee's nightclub less than a mile east, where many guessed Robert Glen Coe bought drugs and became acquainted with the Stouts. It seems now it was our shared corner of the world, mine and Coe's and Cary's.

Meek Street was a row of one-story shacks and trailers,

vicious dogs chained in every yard, the hulls of old cars beached on grassless lawns. A cliché— the one about white Southern poverty. My brother and I took our lumps on the public basketball courts and playgrounds from rough Meek Street boys who resented our clean clothes and shiny new basketballs. We were, in general, mysterious. They called my father "the mad scientist," though he was in fact a professor of English and was, by university professor standards, hardly mad, not even very eccentric.

Leland Bracknell lived in a brown trailer on Meek Street down below our backyard and came to see my mother every morning, knocking on the back door and asking for each one of my mother's children until he discovered one awake. He was my almost constant playmate, and seems to make his way now into everything I write.

I was supposed to spend the night in Leland's trailer once as a little boy. I remember his father, an older man who worked nights at a tool and die, was sleeping on the sofa in the middle of the afternoon. The trailer seemed so narrow, and I smelled the fetid odor of the water heater laboring in a hallway closet. We went to Leland's bedroom and were thumbing through his brother Kevin's KISS albums when I just got the feeling I couldn't be there anymore. I don't know what I was afraid of— poverty maybe. Hopelessness.

Leland was not insulted, but his mother was. "What's wrong, honey?" she said as I walked past her toward the door. She was younger than Leland's father and had some teeth missing. Her eyes said, "What? We're not good enough?" She'd borrowed money from my mother from time to time, was once arrested for shoplifting a can of Aqua Net hairspray from the dime store. I picked up my little suitcase and walked through his backyard to my house. It was still light out. I found my mother smoking under the Magnolia tree in our front yard and cried and cried, though I couldn't tell her why.

As we got older, my brother and friends and I made merciless fun of the Meek Street "chain gangers"— else, my brother says now, we'd have had to acknowledge truths we weren't ready for, the kind of truths that scared and shamed me that night at Leland's. My brother and I did not like the idea that there were boys like Robert Glen Coe still out there, remnants of that sharecropping, Caldwellian Old South, tucked here and there in trailers and ramshackle farmhouses, starving.

*

Willie Coe's abuse intensified as his daughters matured. Both sisters testified at Coe's trial that their father had sexually abused them, forcing the children to watch as he masturbated or exposed himself in public, forcing Robert to watch as he engaged in sex with the older daughter, Bonnie Faye. The girls claim Willie Coe forced his children to watch as Annabelle engaged in sex with other men, even relatives.

As is typical among victims of child sexual abuse, young Robert Glen Coe began to act out. Kathie Parish, married to Coe's older brother Roger from 1967 to 1984, says Robert exposed himself to her when he was ten years old. "It just happened once when he was ten years old," Parish says, "I was never afraid of him." Coe told psychiatrists evaluating him before his trial that he had frequently tried to rape his sisters and cousins, and would likely do so again if released.

Coe often visited his father and sister Bonnie down in Atwood, Tennessee, after his parents' separation, and Dorothy

Cook remembers seeing teenaged Robert standing 100 feet from her as she carried the garbage out to her backyard one afternoon. "I heard a whistle," she told a *Jackson Sun* reporter, "kind of like a bird whistle but I knew it wasn't a bird, so I turned around to look."

"He was standing there," says Cook, who still lives in the same house on Howse Church Road four miles outside of Atwood. "All he was wearing was a red baseball cap and he was, you know, doing it to himself. I was so shocked. It scared me so. No telling how long he was watching me."

*

In 1974 when Coe's 43-year-old mother left Tennessee for Florida with a short order cook from the restaurant where she'd been working (a man 22 years old, hardly older than Robert), Robert went with them. Her friend Kathie Parish says Annabelle Coe was always planning to get Robert to a psychiatrist to get him "cured" but never did. Annabelle enrolled nineteen-year-old Robert in the 10th grade in Immokalee, Florida, but he dropped out not long after.

Florida seems to be where Coe's serious trouble began. He continued to abuse alcohol and marijuana, which he'd done since pre-adolescence, but now Coe also began to experiment with harder drugs, sniffing glue and dropping acid. He later told psychiatrists he joined a cult of "Satan-worshippers" and that he'd participated in the killing of several virginal women, though the psychiatrists expressed serious doubt as to the veracity of these latter claims.

Coe was arrested and charged with attempted sexual battery and aggravated assault after attacking a woman in a trailer park in Collier County, Florida, in January of 1975.

According to court records, he was negotiating the purchase of the trailer from the woman, a woman his mother's age, when he became aroused. She rejected him, he says, laughed at his advances, so he attacked her, stabbing her repeatedly (an oddly prescient episode, as it relates to Coe's version of the Medlin murder).

Florida courts deemed him unfit to stand trial and remanded him to the Florida State Hospital in Chattahoochee for evaluation, where he stayed on and off though 1977. Coe reported auditory and visual hallucinations at the time of admission and was provisionally diagnosed with acute schizophrenic reaction (in remission), chronic schizophrenia (mild to moderate), and sexual deviation. Doctors there noted immediately his flat, inappropriate affect, his general detachment but also the current of anxiety beneath it, the constant, toe-tapping agitation. To a man, doctors considered him a danger to himself and others, and they agreed he was not able to understand the nature and seriousness of his crime.

Coe seemed terrified during the February 1975 interviews, weeping often, particularly when recounting his difficult childhood. He admitted to engaging in bestiality and animal torture as a teenager, to stealing women's underwear from clotheslines for sexual gratification, and to voyeurism and pedophilic urges. He told examiners that he had an aversion to wearing underwear and that during times of stress he felt a strong urge to "flash." He said that sometimes he believed the Devil took over his mind—"I'm over there looking at me do things I don't want to do, but there's nothing I can do about it," he told evaluators.

Doctors were suspicious and found his understanding

of his crimes and his personal history largely superficial, something he used to shock staff and fellow patients in group therapy sessions. Coe participated willingly in substance abuse and sex offender support groups, also in occupational and art therapy, if less wholeheartedly in the latter.

In April of 1975 a doctor reported that he thought Coe exhibited "no treatment potential," expressing frustration that Coe continued to demonstrate impulsive behavior despite consequences, repeatedly exposing himself to female staff members and indulging in angry outbursts, and recommended that he be returned to court for alternative disposition. But by the time of his second evaluation in September of 1975, Coe had begun to show improvement, manifesting less anxiety, confusion, and anger. Doctors were still concerned about what they considered his "borderline" or "dull normal" intelligence and bad judgment, his lack of education and general immaturity, not to mention his denial of his very serious problems ("his thought patterns tend toward blocking," wrote one doctor).

He told one examiner, for example, that he planned to deal with his sexual problems simply by not thinking about sex anymore— the hospital had really helped him learn to do this— and that what he really needed was to get out and find a good job. He had no answer for the doctor who pointed out his spotty employment record and asked why he was so sure his life would be different this time around— Coe had worked as a farmhand, a gas station attendant, and on the assembly line at various local plants, but had never held down any particular job for longer than four months. Officials agreed he still represented a "marked danger" and recommended he remain in the hospital.

By October of 1977, though, doctors decided Coe had, after more than two and a half years in the state hospital, "obtained maximum benefit from inpatient psychiatric hospitalization" and "is much less likely to commit onerous sexual offenses than he once was." Coe was not "cured" (as his mother dreamed he would be), but he was no longer acutely psychotic, according to the report, and did not "have any perceptual distortions like illusions or hallucinations and there is no evidence of overt aggressive impulses." The state was prepared to release him.

Coe's case is not an isolated one. Since John F. Kennedy signed the Community Mental Health Centers Act in 1961, old-fashioned, horror-movie mental hospitals had been emptying out, the number of patients in state and county mental hospitals in this country having peaked at 558,000 in 1955 and dropped to less than 62,000 by 1996. The problem with what some (including New York Democrat Patrick Moynihan, an original signer of the Kennedy legislation) have called the "great liberal mistake" of the mainstreaming of the mentally ill is that, while its altruistic intentions were to end the "labeling" and indiscriminate "drugging" of the mentally ill, the essential effect of this mainstreaming was to leave many mentally ill men and women, those without resources and family support for instance, to fend for themselves, to victimize, and, even more often, be victimized.

A committee of the hospital staff recommended Coe be released to his mother's recognizance, provided Coe agreed to continue to seek professional help with his sexual compulsiveness and exhibitionism and to continue to take his Thorazine, and provided he avoided alcohol and drugs and other known triggers. It seems in hindsight a long list of qualifications and provisions for a man of Coe's limited intelligence and education and considering the home life that likely awaited him in Immokalee with his waitress mother and her new young husband, for a man like Coe who likely walked out into cool Florida liberty planning to ignore all that advice and battle his demons by merely refusing to admit they were there. It seems in hindsight, one has to say, a breathtaking washing of the hands.

Chapter 6:
Bad Desire

Hey little girl, is your daddy home? Did he go
away and leave you all alone?

Bruce Springsteen, "I'm on Fire"

Agents Daniel and Blackwell recorded Robert Glen
Coe's full confession at 7:49 p.m. on the evening of Tuesday,
September 4th, in the conference room of the Weakley County
jail. Coe's answer to Daniel's first question, "What happened
Saturday afternoon concerning a little girl in Greenfield,
Tennessee?" is indiscernible on the audiotape.

"Let me help you," Daniel says to Coe, and help he did,
throughout the confession, as Coe rarely offered more than
one or two word answers to the agent's questions, often
saying he simply didn't know— where he'd picked the girl
up, what time that might have been, what he'd said to her
brother, where he'd killed her, where he'd disposed of the
weapon or the shoes he'd been wearing, why he'd done such
a thing.

Coe said he hadn't gone directly from his home in
McKenzie to Greenfield after work that afternoon but had
stopped in Paris, Tennessee, to "flash."

Daniel: When you left there, where did you go?

Coe: To Gleason.

Daniel: What did you do there?

Coe: Flashed.

Daniel: When you left there, where did you go?

Coe: Greenfield.

Daniel: Greenfield. And what did you do there?

Coe: I killed her.

Coe explained how he'd seen a boy and girl on a neighborhood street there in Greenfield. "I seen her. They was on a bicycle," says Coe. He doesn't recall what he said to entice Cary Ann into his car. "I don't remember what I told her, " he says, "Something about I was looking for her daddy. I thought she would tell that boy to leave."

Daniel: Did the children indicate what direction home might be?

Coe: Yes. But I done forgot where it was.

Daniel: What time was this?

Coe: I'm not sure.

Daniel: Was it before dark?

Coe: Yes.

Daniel: Could you estimate?

Coe: About four o'clock.

Daniel: Could it have been 5:30 or 6?

Coe: Yes.

Coe explains how he left the church parking lot and drove until he found a gravel road. He isn't sure of the direction. "I was pretty high," he says. Perhaps he could help the agents find that gravel road again, the agents suggest.

"She asked me where I was going, and I told her 'for a ride.' She just hung her head down and she did not say anything else," Coe explains in his written statement. "I drove around some streets, and I drove up a gravel road to a ball park and turned around because some cars were parked there. I drove around on some more roads looking for a place to go, and I finally found that gravel road. I did not know that road was there. When I got to the gravel road I just pulled down the road and turned around and stopped. The little girl did not say anything."

Daniel: Could you explain what was at the end of the gravel road?

Coe: It was just at the end of it, coming to some gates at a field.

Daniel: What happened there?

Coe: That's where I done it at.

Daniel: What did you do?

Coe: I raped and killed her.

Daniel: How did you rape her?

Coe: I don't know. I just done it. Well, it wasn't rape; it was with my hands.

Coe explains he'd assaulted the girl in the front seat of his car, and that she remained mostly clothed the whole time. As he masturbated, he says he asked Cary Medlin if she'd ever seen anyone do that before and that she told him she had. It was wrong, she told him, and he shouldn't be doing it. But she never cried. As he climaxed, Coe says he lunged toward the girl and pushed his semen inside her. "I just started shoving it," he told investigators. He claims not to have had anal intercourse with the girl, even when pressed hard on the matter by both Daniel and Blackwell.

"Jesus loves you," Cary Ann Medlin is to have told Robert Glen Coe there in the car. He dragged her from the car then, out onto the grassy roadbed. He was pulling her by the hair of her head and choking her now. "Are you going to kill me?" she asked him. Then he stabbed her in the throat and blood flowed from the wound in her neck "like turning on a hose," Coe would later write in his confession.

"She started jerking and grabbing at her shirt at the neck," Coe wrote. "She struggled and jerked. I got some blood on my hands, and I pulled some leaves off the bushes and wiped the blood on them. Then I ran and tried to get away from there."

Daniel: What did you stab her with?

Coe: I think it was a knife.

Daniel: What kind of knife was it?

Coe: I don't know. Just an old knife.

Daniel: Where did you have that knife?

Coe: I think I got it at the body shop, I don't know.

Daniel: Is it a pocketknife or a straight knife?

Coe: Pocketknife.

Daniel: Where is the knife at now?

Coe: I don't know. I just done it and ran.

Daniel: When she told you Jesus loved you, you killed her? Why did that particular thing make you want to kill her?

Coe: Because it ain't true.

Daniel: Why do you believe that?

76

Coe: I don't know. I just— it's the way things happen, you know. It happens, so I don't care.

Daniel: Why did you want to kill her?

Coe: I don't know. She just said that and…

Daniel: Because she said Jesus loves you?

Coe: I guess. I don't know. I probably would have done it anyway.

Daniel: Now Robert, have we mistreated you in any way while we were talking to you?

Coe: No, sir.

Daniel: Have we made any threats?

Coe: No, sir.

Daniel: Have we made any promises?

Coe: No, sir.

Daniel: This statement was made of your own free will?

Coe: Yes, sir.

Daniel: Alright, then.

*

"Why did that particular thing want to make you kill her?" Agent Daniel asks Coe. Our imaginations, writes James Baldwin, are poorly equipped to accommodate an action we recognize instinctively as "the orgasmic release of self-hatred." We don't understand, and are thus captivated.

I can't help but think of the conclusion of the Flannery O'Connor story "A Good Man Is Hard to Find," where the heroine, the pious, prattling grandmother, faces her own death at the hands of an escaped criminal who calls himself "the Misfit." All alone with him, "nothing around her but woods," she first offers Christian witness to this man who has already shot her son and his young family. "Why don't you pray?" she implores. And when he wants none of it ("Jesus shown everything off balance," he tells her) she extends herself to him. "Why you're one of my babies, you're one of my own children," she says, reaching out to touch him on the shoulder. But the Misfit recoils, "as if a snake had bitten him," writes O'Connor, and shoots the grandmother three times through her chest. Another orgasmic release of self-hatred.

Over the years members of her family and of the media have pointed to the last few moments of Cary Medlin's life as the moment of her martyrdom. At the hour of her death, the most significant in the life of a Christian, Cary shines. "Jesus loves you," she says. It's hard to believe a girl so young could be so self-possessed, though they said that about Anne Frank, too, and yet Otto Frank defended her diary until his death, the manuscript passing test after test for authenticity.

I still have questions about the end of Cary's story, not its authenticity so much as the prevailing interpretations. After all, our source, our only witness, is Coe, otherwise considered such an untrustworthy figure, a con man. And Tennessee Death Row inmate Phillip Workman, executed in 2007 for killing a police officer during a hold-up at a Nashville Wendy's restaurant, pointed to Cary's sentiments: she was not asking for mercy but *offering* it, though few have ever managed to hear that. She had more mercy than a whole state, Workman told a reporter in the days before the Coe execution.

*

The following morning, Wednesday, September 5th, Coe accompanied the arresting officers as they retraced the route he claims he took during the abduction and murder, stopping first at Crestview Motors so Coe could identify the Gran Torino as his car and so police could dust its passenger door for prints. Coe had been housed secretly in the Obion County jail, for his own safety, and as the police caravan moved from the car lot in Gleason to the murder site in Greenfield, authorities rotated Coe from patrol car to patrol car to obscure his exact whereabouts from the curious. He led them to places where he may have tossed his shoes and the pocketknife, though neither was ever recovered.

Coe was arraigned at the Weakley County Courthouse in Dresden at 10 a.m. on Friday the 7th, before Weakley County General Sessions judge Robert Neal Glasgow. Spectators packed the thirty-year-old limestone courthouse for the proceeding, filling the courtroom and marble outer hallways. The county's largest ever security detail— TBI agents, sheriff's deputies, city police and constables— frisked everyone entering the building for weapons, and snipers were even posted on the courthouse roof. Since the time of his arrest, citizens had awaited him outside the jail, jeering. Locals still consider it a wonder he made it to trial without being killed Oswald-style.

Cameras were prohibited inside the courtroom, where Coe told Judge Glasgow he could not afford an attorney. Glasgow then appointed Dresden lawyer Max Speight to the post. Coe wore the same blue mesh #50 football jersey he'd had on since his arrest, staring at the floor through most of the proceeding, except when he turned to stare at Charlotte Stout, seated in the front row.

Because he said he considered Coe a flight risk and a danger to himself and others, the judge denied bail, but Speight immediately requested Coe be evaluated at the Northwest Tennessee Mental Health Center in Martin and moved to another location for his own safety, so Glasgow ordered him moved to Fort Pillow State Prison pending trial. District Attorney General David Hayes told reporters he would seek the death penalty in the case.

In December, a Weakley County Grand Jury returned indictments charging Robert Glen Coe with aggravated rape, aggravated kidnapping, and first-degree murder.

Max Speight countered immediately by moving for a change of venue. Bruce Conley was appointed Obion County attorney, and within a few weeks the defense team had also moved to suppress Coe's post-arrest statements (his confession the only solid evidence police have ever really had) and to dismiss the charges against him on the grounds that the grand jury selection had been illegal (District Attorney David Hayes had been present for the process) and that the death penalty was unconstitutional (Tennessee had not executed anyone since an East Tennessee man named Lawrence Tines was electrocuted in 1960).

*

Annabelle Coe attended one of the team's first meetings at Bruce Conley's law offices in Union City, eager to hear the strategy for getting her son acquitted. She believed him to be innocent, arguing until her death in 1999 that Robert was a good boy. Conley remembers it was difficult to tell her "there was more than sufficient evidence" to convince his defense team that Robert was "very definitely involved in the killing of that little girl." The team, he says, was just trying to save the man's life.

Coe was not well— on the afternoon of his preliminary hearing in September when the Grand Jury had bound him over for trial, a sheriff's deputy had also served him papers there in the courtroom notifying him that his wife Tammy had filed for divorce. Coe and Tammy Forrest had met in 1977 just after Coe had returned to McKenzie, Tennessee, from Florida and married after only three weeks, and her betrayal devastated him. He wrote her long letters from jail, begging her to take him back (she later turned them over to authorities) and it is said that even in his final days Coe longed to be reunited with Tammy and their daughter Rebecca. "Coe shed the apparent calmness he had shown in previous questioning, " wrote a *Weakley County Press* reporter, "and broke into audible sobs at the table with his attorney."

The Court denied all motions to quash the charges against Coe in April of 1980 but in May of that year did grant the motion for change of venue, moving the trial immediately west to Obion County and the court of Hon. Arthur Naquin, Jr. (Weakley County judge Phil B. Harris had recused himself because he lived so near the Stout family), and jury selection began at the Obion County Courthouse on May 20, 1980. The prosecutors tried to seat more than 250 different prospective jurors but could find none without prior knowledge of Coe or his alleged crimes. "He had name recognition like Jesus Christ," a lawyer told me several years ago. And not in a good way, I took him to mean, the widespread public enmity for Coe having persisted now thirty years and more. The judge and prosecutors finally gave up after a full week of *voire dire*. The court granted the second change on June 5, 1980, this time 120 miles south of Greenfield to Memphis.

The move gave Max Speight, a self-proclaimed old-fashioned "country lawyer" whose expertise lay in real estate and bankruptcy and who had been a reluctant participant all along, the chance to bow out with head high, and he did, handing the case over to Memphis attorneys James O. Marty and his partner Frank Holloman. Speight had paid a high price— locals say his time as Coe's solicitor ruined his law practice and cost him thousands, and when contacted about this book he asked to be spared even remembering his involvement.

Faced with the government's strong circumstantial case, bolstered importantly by Coe's oral and written confessions, Marty and Holloman sensed right away the same dearth of effective defense options that had faced Speight and Conley. The Memphis firm was sufficiently convinced by Coe's claims that he had been part of a satanic cult in Florida and that the Devil still sometimes "took over his mind"— and apparently sufficiently desperate— that they seriously considered incorporating an exorcism into Coe's defense strategy, even contacting a Roman Catholic priest about the demonic possession theory and the need to exorcise the spirits Coe blamed for his behavior. "Robert indicated he was a Satan worshiper, and he was adamant about it," James Marty told Memphis *Commercial Appeal* writer Lawrence Buser in the days leading up to Coe's execution. Coe said during one pretrial psychological evaluation that he had turned to Satan because he felt abandoned by God, that he was angry with God for allowing his father Willie to treat him the way he had. "I didn't know much about the occult, and we were checking out every option we could to help Robert," Marty told Buser. "It was just bizarre."

In the end, Marty and Holloman abandoned the demonic possession theory for a more conventional insanity defense. After all, Florida mental health officials had deemed Coe unfit to stand trial only five years before, and the circumstances of the two crimes, the attack on the Florida woman and Cary Medlin's murder, had been similar, at least as far as Coe's state of mind was concerned (he claimed to be under the influence of L.S.D. and suffering from auditory hallucinations in both instances). It seemed as good a bet as any. Yet it was perhaps the differences in the cases that are telltale: unlike little Cary Medlin, the woman in Florida had survived.

Coe had been subject to a seemingly endless series of mental health evaluations since his arrest in September of 1979, but in January of 1981 Shelby County judge William H. Williams convened defense and state experts to determine once and for all Coe's fitness to stand trial. Attorneys and mental health professionals would apply what are known as the McNaughton Rule to establish a potential excuse for Coe from criminal liability. Established by the British House of Lords in 1843, when satisfied they provide the accused with a special "not guilty by reason of insanity" plea, the sentence for which is either a mandatory or indeterminate stay in a secure hospital facility, depending on the country. The test's interest is in the accused's state of mind at the time he committed the offense; whether he knew that what he was doing would have an illegal outcome; and whether the accused was afflicted, at least temporarily with a "disease of the mind" or was impaired by a "defect of reason."

Interestingly, the Rules establish insanity in a strictly legal and not psychological sense, and they remain unchanged despite advances in psychology and neuroscience in the more than 150 years since they were first invoked. Defendants suffering from ailments as various as arteriosclerosis, diabetes, and epilepsy have been granted McNaughton's "disease of the mind" protection on the assumption that their conditions led to an automatism that rendered them irresponsible for their actions (the arteriosclerotic smote his wife with a hammer, the diabetic stole a car while in hypoglycemic shock), yet courts have not recognized clinical depression and anxiety disorders, what we conventionally consider true diseases of the brain, as eligible for these protections.

By these standards, neither Coe's seemingly verifiable mental illness nor his auditory hallucinations seemed to provide him with exemption from prosecution. In the United States, persons acting under what McNaughton terms "insane delusions" are still punishable provided they understand they are acting contrary to law. A man who cuts his wife's throat, for example, is legally sane and fit to stand trial in American courts if he recognizes it was actually his wife's throat he was cutting and does not think he was slicing a loaf of bread and so long as he understood the act was against the law, even if he was convinced God himself had told him to cut his wife's throat.

While doctors in Florida who examined Coe in the mid-seventies had sometimes disagreed about the course of his treatment, they remained unanimous in their finding that Coe was mentally ill and unfit for criminal trial. But the nature of the Medlin murder and the fact that Coe's was a capital murder trial meant the question of his legal sanity was a great deal more hotly contested in Memphis in January of 1981 than it had been in Florida.

James Marty read into the medical records and reports from Coe's period of incarceration in Florida, then called to the stand expert witnesses to speak to Coe's mental competency. Defense expert Dr. Allen O. Battle, a clinical psychologist, testified that he had observed Coe in May of 1980 and again in January of 1981 and that he had administered a battery of psychological tests on both occasions. Wexler intelligence tests showed that Coe's I.Q. had dropped from the dull normal range (98) to mentally retarded range (70) during the time between examinations and the Rorschach ink blot test revealed in Coe some personality disorganization and psychotic thinking. "Robert is the most pathetic person I have ever seen," Dr. Battle told the court, reflecting on the rejection Coe had suffered all his life. It was Battle's conclusion that the defendant did suffer from a mental disorder and would not have been able to conform his conduct to the requirements alone, that Coe's drug use alone would have rendered him psychotic on the day of the Medlin murder, though he conceded on cross examination that Coe's drug use was voluntary and that he understood at all times the wrongfulness of his actions.

Psychiatrist David Cook testified that, based upon his examinations, Coe was a paranoid schizophrenic and that this condition was drug-induced and drug-aggravated. Like Battle, Cook determined that Coe would likely not have been able to conform his behavior to the requirements of the law, yet on cross examination he admitted to prosecutor David Hayes that such a determination was only a "guess."

District Attorney Hayes believed Coe suffered not from

a disease of the mind, as he would later tell jurors, but from a disease of the heart. He was not crazy but evil. Assisted by Shelby County prosecutor Leland McNabb, Hayes countered defense insanity claims with testimony from experts like clinical psychologist Dr. Nicholas House, III, who had observed Coe during the month Coe spent at the Western State Mental Health Institute in Bolivar, Tennessee, the year prior to the Coe murder, after Coe had been picked up for indecent exposure in McKenzie (this 1978 arrest was the first Coe's new wife, Tammy, had heard of his "flashing" problem). Dr. House reported that he had conducted many of the same tests defense experts had conducted and that Coe had tested in the "normal" range in every instance. House said Coe exhibited no indication of psychosis and suffered from no serious mental disorders, and that based on a review of all mental health records, state's evidence, and on conversations with other examining physicians, he had determined that Coe was not insane on September 1, 1979, nor on any other day.

Dr. John Gonzales, who examined Coe at the Mental Health Center in Martin, Tennessee, in 1979, concurred with Dr. House, as did Dr. John Robert Hutson. Clinical psychologist Dr. Robert Glen Watson went so far as to suggest that Coe was not only competent to stand trial but that Coe had manipulated tests in order to appear schizophrenic. "He was consciously trying to present himself as sick and disturbed," Watson testified.

Coe's attorneys reported to Judge Williams that one state expert had tried to intimidate Coe during a psychological evaluation, that Coe was frightened of the doctor, who indicated that he would ensure Robert paid for what he had done to that little girl. But Judge Williams turned a deaf ear to defense complaints, saying he had known the psychiatrist in question for more than twenty years and refused to believe the doctor would do such a thing. On January 20, 1981, Williams declared Coe fit to stand trial, and jury selection began the following day. Prosecutor McNabb gloated years later that Coe had been able to fool doctors in the short run but that "his 30-day act was not so good."

Chapter 7:
Frailty of Human Memory

Altogether, there were seventeen prints, and as they were passed from hand to hand, the jurors' expressions reflected the impact the pictures made: one man's cheeks reddened, as if he had been slapped, and a few, after the first distressing glance, obviously had no heart for the task; it was as though the photographs had pried open their mind's eye and forced them to at last really see the true and pitiful thing that had been done to a neighbor and his wife and children. It amazed them, it made them angry, and several of them... stared at the defendants with total contempt.

Truman Capote, In Cold Blood

Robert Glen Coe's capital murder trial began on February 17, 1981, in the Shelby County Courthouse on Adams Avenue in the heart of downtown Memphis, Judge Williams presiding, with Coe entering a "not guilty" plea. Reading transcripts of the trial, I imagine the turn of the twentieth century courthouse, later used as a set in films like *The Firm* and *The Silence of the Lambs*, must have seemed an intimidating place to God-fearing people like Jerry Medlin and the Stout family— its curved marble staircases and mahogany banisters, the six immense marble statues adorning its limestone façade invoking Justice, Authority,

Liberty, Peace, Prosperity, and Wisdom.

Charlotte Stout was first to take the stand, District Attorney David Hayes asking her what she remembered about the last time she saw Cary Ann. She said it had been just an ordinary Saturday, that she saw Cary and Michael head out the door to ride bikes and she reminded them of the bike-riding rules and that supper would be ready soon.

Hayes asked her what Cary had been wearing that afternoon and wanted her to identify the clothes in some photographs Hayes wanted to introduce, photographs from the murder scene. James Marty raised an objection to introducing the gruesome photos so early, but Williams said it established *corpus delicti* (the existence of a corpse proving a crime had actually been committed) and overruled him. Hayes then had Charlotte Stout identify Cary Ann's belongings— the wooden-soled sandals, her bloody clothes. Marty objected, again in vain, to the introduction of bloody clothes, which Hayes took from sealed plastic evidence bags. Hayes had Mrs. Stout identify her house and that of her in-laws on an aerial photograph of Greenfield, then turned her over to James Marty for cross-examination.

Charlotte Stout was curt with Coe's attorney. "Do you know whether or not Cary and Michael went over to the Stouts' home behind yours that afternoon?" Marty asked her.

"How would I know that?" she said.

Marty led her through another recounting of the afternoon of September 1, 1979, but her answers were not generous ones, usually only a word or two.

"Now, have you ever met Robert Glen Coe?" Marty asked Mrs. Stout. "Did you know him prior—"

"Prior to this?" she interrupted.

"Did you know Robert Glen Coe prior to September 1, 1979?" Marty asked her.

"No, I did not," she told him.

"Did your husband know him, as far as you know?" Marty asked. "Did your husband know Robert Glen Coe before September 1, 1979?"

"I don't know," said Stout.

Charlotte Stout denied having ever met Coe's friend Daryl Ross, or his purported drug contact Jack Lynch. Marty told the court he had no further questions, but just as Charlotte Stout prepared to leave the stand, Marty thought of one more.

"Did you know a John Sands prior to September 1, 1979?" Marty asked her. This was a new name.

"Not that I recall," she said.

Memphis prosecutor Leland McNabb took over for Hayes and called Cary's father Jerry Lynn Medlin to the stand, and McNabb asked Medlin to identify himself and what he did for a living. Medlin explained he worked as an avionics technician at Memphis Aero.

"The only thing I know about airplanes is that they have wings," McNabb confessed, "What is an avionics technician?"

"I work on the computers that fly airplanes," Medlin told him. "It's called autopilot."

Jerry Medlin explained that because of his father's illness, he had not seen his daughter in the six weeks prior to her death. He described, over James Marty's objections, hearing on a police scanner that searchers had found Cary Ann's body, then going down to Bean Switch Road to identify her. McNabb had him look at a photograph, state's exhibit 53.

"Does the photograph depict, in part, how your daughter

appeared at the time you saw her out there?" McNabb asked him.

"No," Medlin answered, "it looked like her, but it was more— Do you want me to tell what I saw?"

"No sir," McNabb said. "Just that that was your daughter. Thank you."

McNabb asked if Medlin had ever met Robert Glen Coe and whether Medlin knew if Coe had anything against him, but Medlin said he'd never met nor heard of Coe.

McNabb asked Medlin about Cary's sandals and her father told the court he remembers her trying to run while wearing them, how she "would either trip or run out of them." He told the court he knew Cary Ann regularly attended Sunday school but that he did not know her to be in the habit of making religious statements on the order of "Jesus loves you."

Leland McNabb next called one of his eyewitnesses, Cary Ann's step-grandmother Maggie Lee Stout, to the stand. She told the court about watching Cary and Michael from her kitchen window as the two-tone brown Torino approached, about the man inside, who she admits she saw "only slightly."

"Can you describe the position of the occupant of the automobile when you looked out the window?" McNabb asked her.

"I could see the side of his face."

McNabb offered photographs in an attempt to establish the distance between the Stouts' kitchen window and the place in the street where the Torino idled the afternoon of the murder. Maggie Stout told McNabb she could not be certain the defendant was the man she'd seen in the car.

James Marty zeroed in on Maggie Stout's doubt in his cross-examination. Marty asked her about the initial description of Cary's killer— a young man with a thin, ugly face and dirty, neck-length brownish-blond hair— which she had offered to Agent Alvin Daniel at 11:05 p.m. on the night of the abduction, an interview she claimed not to remember.

"You don't remember anything about that?" Marty asked.

"I sure don't," she told him.

Maggie Stout conceded that she and her grandson had viewed a line-up and identified a man, standing in the #4 spot in the line-up, who was not Robert Glen Coe.

"I will ask you this," Marty said, "That individual right there, Mr. Robert Glen Coe, didn't stand in front of you at that line-up, did he?"

"No, sir."

"But you picked someone out, didn't you?" Marty pressed her.

"Yes," she said.

Marty then offered the litany of names he read to each prosecution witness:

Lynch, Ross, Sands. She said she knew none of them, and that her husband, Joe, seated in the courtroom, had never mentioned any of them to her.

Marty seemed to sneak his final question, a provocation, a sucker punch.

"Isn't it a fact that you deal in drugs at your establishment?" Marty asked Maggie Stout. Early in her testimony, he'd had her establish that she owned an eponymous nightclub that sold alcohol.

"Your honor, we are going to object to that," David Hayes

said to Williams.

Williams sustained the objection. "Ladies and Gentlemen, the law in Tennessee is that this is an improper question in the manner in which it was asked," the judge told jurors. "So, the truth or veracity of this witness is not jeopardized by that question. Please proceed on, Mr. Marty."

But the defense strategy was becoming clear. There was a persistent rumor in the months after the crime that Cary's murder had been linked to a drug trade that ran out of "Maggie Lee's." Coe, some suggested, had been a former customer, frozen out by the Stouts for money owed— it would explain Coe's apparent familiarity with Mickey Stout. If Marty could get that in front of a jury, along with the names of sketchy characters like Ross and Lynch and the mysterious Sands, and if he could cast doubt upon the eyewitness identifications of Coe, it might be seed for reasonable doubt. Maybe Coe's attorneys wouldn't need to rely, as many speculated they would, solely on an insanity defense. "The State of Tennessee wants you to authorize it to kill Robert Glen Coe," defense attorney Diane Spears had said in her opening remarks, "you can't do that on the frailties of human memory."

David Hayes called and questioned the next eyewitness, Cary Medlin's stepbrother Michael Stout. Hayes led Michael, eight years old by the time of the trial, through the bike ride he and Cary had taken that Saturday eighteen months before. A man in a car, Michael testified, had seen the two children riding in the Primitive Baptist Church parking lot and turned around to follow them. Michael remembered the car was not brown on brown, as his grandmother had suggested, but grayish green with a black top. He identifies the defendant, Robert Glen Coe, as the man he'd seen Cary ride away with that day.

"Do you see him in the courtroom today?" Hayes asks him. "The man who took Cary away?"

"Um-Hum," Michael Stout answers.

"Are you sure of that?" says Hayes.

"Um-hum."

"You are absolutely positive you see that person?"

"Yes, sir."

"Would you point him out," Hayes asks.

"Right over there," Michael tells the court, pointing to Coe.

"Nothing further, your honor," says Hayes.

"I am a lawyer. Do you know that?" James Marty asks Michael Stout, to begin his cross-examination of the boy.

"No," Michael tells him.

"I have to ask you some questions," Marty explains. He asks if parents, prosecutors, or police have said anything to him about his testimony.

"They just told me not to be scared— and I am— and I forgot the other one," the boy says. Laughter spreads across the courtroom.

"Do you know what it means to tell a lie?" Marty asks the boy. "What happens to people who tell lies?"

Michael looks sheepishly at his family and points at his shoes, at the floor. "They go down there," he says.

He tells James Marty he remembers the man who took Cary had "yellowish" hair, blonde like Marty's hair but even whiter. Marty asks him to describe the color of Coe's hair. "Brownish-black," he says. He admitted that, like his grandmother, he had identified a man other than Coe in an earlier police line-up as the one who had abducted Cary.

The state next called Stout neighbor Herbert Clements next, who identified a photograph of Cary Ann as the girl he'd seen in the Gran Torino on a Saturday afternoon a year and a half before. But like Maggie Stout and her grandson, he too struggled to positively identify Coe as the man he saw driving the car he saw whisking Cary Ann out of town— Cary sat in the Torino's passenger seat between Clements and her killer.

Yet if the defense team was encouraged by the testimony of Cary Ann's family, believed they might have planted seeds of doubt about dubious eyewitness identifications of Coe and her grandparents' position as pillars of the community, they had to be discouraged by the testimony Coe's wife and close friends offered. And if the Stouts had seemed intimidated by the giant hall of justice, Coe's cohort seemed positively witless and absolutely terrified.

When Leland McNabb called Robert Glen Coe's former brother-in-law Donald Box to the stand and asked him to state and spell his name, Box did so dutifully.

"Mr. Box," McNabb told him, "you talk pretty fast and fairly soft. This young lady over here is writing down everything you say," said McNabb, pointing to the court reporter, "and I want you to make sure that all of the jurors can hear you."

Box told the court how Robert Glen Coe seemed scared the night of Cary Ann's murder, hurried. He didn't eat, though he was usually a chowhound, and he complained of head and stomach pain, even said to Box he'd be "better off dead" when he couldn't get his Torino to turn over.

Donald Box's wife, Vickie, also testified that Coe seemed

upset, "a little depressed," and that she gave him a muscle relaxer for his discomfort. Sixteen-year-old Coe family friend Janet Ross told McNabb that Coe was an "average everyday person" but that he seemed "scared and nervous and upset and everything" when he stopped by her house in Big Buck the morning after Cary Medlin had disappeared. Mrs. Ross repeated the story Coe had told her about his run-in with State Troopers in Camden. Janet Ross went on to describe the dye job she'd given Coe, Coe's attempt to purchase a gun from her father-in-law, his several trips to the bus station to procure Greyhound tickets to Georgia.

Darrell Ross, Janet's 21-year-old husband, seemed to struggle with McNabb's simplest questions. "Do you live in a regular or a mobile home," McNabb asked early in Ross's testimony.

"Regular. A mobile home," Ross said.

"On September 1, 1979, did you or did you not have a beard?" McNabb asked him.

"Yes," Ross answered.

"I am not intending to embarrass you by asking this," McNabb told Ross, "but how far did you get in school?"

"Eighth grade," Ross told him. His wife had reported she'd only finished seventh grade before getting pregnant.

"Can you read?" McNabb asked Ross.

"No, sir," Ross answered.

"Can you write?" McNabb asked.

"I can sign a check," Ross said.

McNabb was careful to have Janet Ross describe the stab wound Coe claimed he'd given the trooper, in the neck, precisely where Cary Medlin had been stabbed. He was also careful to establish among all those who had seen Coe on the day of the murder that, though very upset, he did not seem drunk or high. Martin exterminator Freddie Harelson testified that he'd seen Coe on the day of the murder, at the home of his wife's sister Edith Poore on Meek Street in Martin, and that Coe did not seem intoxicated, despite defense claims.

The prosecutors also had interest in preventing any "defect of reason" claims from the defense. "As far as Robert Coe's intelligence," prosecutor David Hayes asked Harelson, "would you say he is retarded or intelligent?" Marty objected on the grounds that Harelson wasn't qualified to make such a determination, but Judge Williams ruled the man could certainly determine whether a man was "quick or slow.'"

"I'd heard he was weird," Harelson told the court. "I'd say he was as smart as I am. I wouldn't call him an idiot, I wouldn't call him a genius."

TBI agent Alvin Daniels spent more of the week-long trial on the stand than any other witness, leading jurors through the state's history of the case from the time he first responded to the call from the Stout home all the way to Coe's arrest, and after, when he and Blackwell and sheriff's deputies had Coe lead them to where he'd dumped the murder weapon. Jurors heard an audiotape of Coe's confession and a report on the autopsy from the Memphis pathologist and serologist, and TBI agents accounted for the evidence's "chain of custody."

*

As defense proof, James Marty offered the testimony of the three psychiatrists who argued that Robert Glen Coe was in fact mentally ill on the day of the murder and therefore unable to conform to the law, which McNabb's experts rebutted in turn. The testimony of Coe's ex-wife Tammy Forrest Coe Hopper (she'd re-married in the time between Coe's arrest and his trial and had changed baby Rebecca's name and sent her away to live with relatives) was perhaps the most damning of the trial. Though she admitted to defense attorney Diane Spears that she felt somewhat intimidated by authorities early on (she says Agents Daniel and Blackwell threatened to jail her on conspiracy charges and take her daughter away the night of her ex-husband's arrest), she ultimately proved a useful rebuttal witness, telling prosecutors that Coe did not seem drunk nor high when she saw him on September 1, 1979 (though she'd remarked in earlier statements how he seemed to be coming down off a high). She said she'd never known him to experience drug-induced flashbacks or blackouts (though Coe wrote jailhouse letters to Tammy claiming all he could remember about the murder was that he'd done it). She also reported that Coe had once boasted that he could "wrap [psychiatrists] around his little finger."

Tammy Hopper said that she was aware of Coe's flashing problem but believed his stay at the mental hospital in November of the year before the murder had cured him.

"Were you and Robert having marital problems?" James Marty asked Tammy Hopper during rebuttal questioning.

"Not that I knew of," she told him. "We had fights. He beat me."

During the final days of the trial, some in the press speculated that Coe's defense team might try to change course, move away from the contested insanity claims and establish Coe as having been somewhere else on the afternoon of the murder— apparently defense attorney Diane Spears had made references to that effect in the courtroom. But Marty called only Coe's sisters to establish the horrors of his childhood.

Billie Jean Mayberry [then Tolley], the sister closest in age to Robert Glen Coe, reported that the two were "mostly raised up together." "We was the same age to play together, you know," she told Marty. Tolley says she witnessed her father's sexual abuse: "he would make us, me and Robert, stand there while he raped my sister Bonnie," she said. And her father had beaten the boy regularly. "He would beat Robert, I think," she testified, "just for the fun of it." She said she had known Robert to sniff paint fumes and to smoke marijuana cigarettes, that her husband had even smoked with him before.

Leland McNabb pointed out on cross-examination that the 23-year-old Mrs. Tolley and her husband still lived with Willie Coe in a modest house in Atwood, Tennessee, where he had lived since his divorce from Annabelle.

"After these things you've just described, you still live with your father?" asked the prosecutor.

"Yes, but he's different," she said of her father. "He's a whole different person. He's not drinking anymore and we believe the reason he did those things was because he drank all the time which he doesn't no more. The only thing he drinks now is mostly coffee."

McNabb did not cross-examine Billie Jean's sister Bonnie Faye Deshields [then Pollock]. In emotional direct testimony the *Weakley County Press* called a "surprise," Bonnie Pollock of Hornbeak in Obion County, Tennessee, the sister who had first tipped police about her brother and his whereabouts, revealed the incest and sexual abuse in the Coe home.

"I don't remember any earlier, but it was earlier than when I was seven years old," she told James Marty, fighting tears. "But I know that when I was seven that my daddy had raped me before this." She said he'd done it more than once. Prosecutors declined to question the 26-year-old Pollock, and she began to heave and sob as she left the stand.

Coe's Meek Street cousin Edith Poore was Marty's final witness, one more attempt to establish Coe's intoxication. She testified that she'd seen Robert ingest "five star blotter acid" and smoke at least three joints on Friday, August 31st, and that he visited her home to take drugs at least once a week in those days, sometimes twice. She said she believed it possible that Coe could have been high well into the day of the murder, based on what he'd licked, drunk, and inhaled. "I've did kinds," she said of the acid she and Coe had shared that Friday evening, "to where I'd sit and watch the ashtray melt."

But McNabb swooped in to discredit her on cross. "Mrs. Poore, isn't it true that you have a hard time remembering any dates because of the fact that you've taken so many drugs?" he asks her. "Am I not correct in that?"

"Well, I don't know that for sure," Poore replied. "I can remember stuff. I can't remember everything."

Marty rested his defense. As expected, the state had presented a strong if very circumstantial case: impeachable eyewitnesses, pre-DNA physical evidence not actually linked to the defendant, a disavowed confession. Marty had done a passably good job of exploiting these holes in the prosecution's case, but his insanity strategy, established on the grounds either that Coe was acutely mentally ill or that he was intoxicated on the evening of the murder (or both), seemed to gain little purchase within the courtroom or without. In the end he had, with the testimony of Coe's sisters, thrown his client upon the jurors' mercy.

Robert Glen Coe had elected not to testify on his own behalf. When Judge Williams first attempted to confirm that this was indeed Coe's decision, counsel informed the judge that the defendant had purchased Valium from fellow inmates in the Shelby County lock-up, had crushed five tablets and swallowed them and so was not sufficiently coherent to provide such a confirmation. When brought back before the judge the following morning, Coe said again that he did not wish to testify.

"Have we in any way coerced you into making that decision?" James Marty asked him.

"What does that mean?" Coe replied.

"Have we tried to influence your decision one way or the other?" Marty explained.

"I don't know," Coe told the court, "I just don't want to do it."

*

David Hayes offered the prosecution's closing argument, claiming the state's case had revealed Coe to be a man with "a calculating, thinking, planning brain who is not mentally diseased," who can "avoid and evade detection" and "has caused some very fine people up there in northwest Tennessee to spend a bunch of sleepless nights in a little bitty town."

"Oh, no," Hayes told jurors, "Robert Glen Coe is guilty, I submit to you, of the offense of murder in the first degree. He is guilty of aggravated rape, and commenced it with aggravated kidnapping."

"I ask you, ladies and gentlemen," intoned Hayes, "to convict this man who rises from the bottom and grabs prey like a gray shark"— and here Hayes steals shamelessly from the Robbie Dupree song "Hot Rod Hearts," on Billboard charts at the time of the trial—"up from the bottom for another bite."

In his close, James Marty all but acquiesced to the verdict, but he again asked jurors to consider mitigating factors, to act with mercy. "Is Robert a cruel person?" asked Marty. "Is he a wicked person? " "No," Marty said, "Robert Coe is a derelict. He needs to go to jail, but he doesn't need to die."

"It's a tough decision," Marty told jurors. "One I couldn't make. Robert thinks God hates him. He's sure you hate him. I'm asking that you give him something no one else has ever given him. Give him life. Give him life."

But Hayes was relentless. Earlier in the *voire dire*, some jurors had expressed reluctance to serve on the jury in a capital case but said they would pray on the matter. When Marty had concluded his opening salvo, Hayes approached the jurors again. "I think that [praying] is the most appropriate thing you can do in this circumstance," Hayes told the jury, "Religious beliefs are in no way inconsistent with a request for capital punishment."

"I'm not a biblical scholar," Hayes said, "and don't pretend to be. But I would simply emphasize to you that the whole cornerstone of our law, the law of this land, the law of society is based upon those scriptures, replete with those circumstances where capital punishment had been applied. Whosoever sheddeth a man's blood, so shall his blood by man be shed. Whatsoever a man soweth, that he shall also reap, ladies and gentlemen, and I think Robert Glen Coe has reaped the whirlwind in this case."

"Be true to your conscience," Hayes instructed them. "Be true to God. It seems to me that every time we have heard the name Robert Glen Coe and his actions, we've started looking for excuses, excuses, excuses. That's all we've heard so far. Well, the excuses have run out."

"The time is drawing nigh to reach this decision, ladies and gentlemen," Hayes told them, "and I ask you, and this may sound harsh, but I ask you in your deliberations, I ask you to show the same mercy to Robert Glen Coe that he showed to Cary Medlin. Because he has placed himself in that chair. You haven't placed him there. I haven't placed him. And you should feel no burden or no responsibility."

*

Newspapers reported that when the jury returned a "guilty" verdict on all three counts that afternoon, Coe threw his head back and laughed. But when he heard his mother weeping in the gallery, he searched the crowd for her face, then put a finger to his lips and mouthed, "I'm sorry."

Prosecutors offered no proof during the penalty phase. The defense only recalled mental health experts to testify again to Coe's incompetence to stand trial in the first place. "Robert is the most pathetic person I've ever seen," Dr. Allen Battle again told the court.

When Judge William H. Williams read Coe's sentence, a life term each for kidnapping and rape, execution in the electric chair for the first degree murder conviction, Coe asked the judge if he could serve the life terms first.

"You will, son," Williams told him. "You will."

Cary Medlin, 2nd Grade.   Robert Glen Coe, 4th Grade.

the author, 2nd grade.
(see page 25)

Robert Glen Coe mug shot, September 4, 1979.
State of Tennessee, used by permission

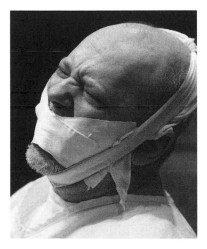

"You can put all the restraints you want on me, I can still holler," Coe yelled in a Memphis courtroom during a mental competency hearing in January of 2000.

Photo by A.J. Wolfe for the Memphis *Commercial Appeal*

Coe's Gran Torino.

State of Tennessee,
used by permission

The Gran Torino
as it would
have appeared
to Maggie Lee
Stout moving
south down
Fairlane Drive on
September 1, 1979.

State of Tennessee,
used by permission

Bean Switch Road.

State of Tennessee,
used by permission

Aerial view of the crime scene outside Greenfield, Tennessee, looking east. The parked car marks the entrance to Bean Switch Road.

State of Tennessee, used by permission

Aerial view of Bean Switch Road, looking north. The parked patrol car and arrow mark the spot where Cary Medlin's body was found.

State of Tennessee, used by permission

Cary Ann Medlin's sandals, wooden-soled with white leather straps, found a few feet from her body on Bean Switch Road.

State of Tennessee, used by permission

Trampled swath of weeds where Cary Medlin's body lay.

State of Tennessee, used by permission

The old gate on Bean Switch Road near where the body was found.

State of Tennessee, used by permission

Sheriff's deputy
examines the
crime scene.

State of Tennessee,
used by permission

Swath of weeds,
Bean Switch Road.

State of Tennessee,
used by permission

Sheriff Marlind
Gallimore and a
Weakley County
Sheriff's Deputy
at the crime scene
(Bean Switch Road).

State of Tennessee,
used by permission

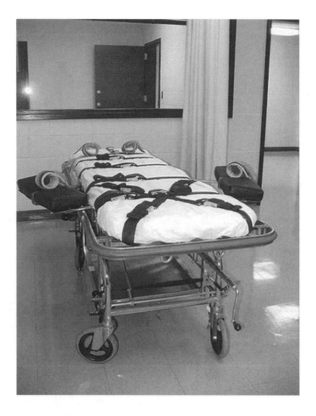

A view of the death chamber at Riverbend Maximum Security Institution in Nashville. The gurney used to hold Robert Glen Coe while he awaited and received a lethal injection is front and center. The observation room where Coe's family watched is visible to the rear. (The Medlin and Stout families, media and other observers viewed the execution from a room to the right, and the executioner worked from a room to the left).

Photo by Clint Confehr

Chapter 8:
History of Violence

It is not so easy to follow a story occurring in one's own country from the vantage of another one. From afar, one may imagine that one perceives a pattern. And one may… as one is not challenged— or, more precisely, menaced— by the details… And after all, what I remembered— or imagined myself to remember— of my life in America (before I left home!) was terror. And what I am trying to suggest by what one imagines oneself to be able to remember is that terror cannot be remembered. One blots it out. The organism— the human being— blots it out.

James Baldwin, Preface to *Evidence of Things Not Seen*

As a boy I never let myself imagine for very long one of my mother's children being snatched up that September day in 1979, perhaps believing such a thing impossible.

I think of the Discovery Channel's "Shark Week" footage of Australian bathers enjoying the surf, waving at the cameraman in the hovering helicopter unaware that a dozen or more bull sharks lurk only yards away, clearly visible from above.

My parents had relocated to Tennessee in 1970, fleeing New Haven in the wake of Black Panther Bobby Seale's controversial murder trial there, figuring the rural south was a safer place to raise a growing family. May Day riots on the New Haven Green had forced my mother's Yale Medical Center obstetrician to cancel several prenatal visits (she was carrying yours truly) and Quinnipiac College, where my parents taught, had cancelled classes as National Guard tanks rolled in to protect the city. So as soon as I was old enough to travel, my parents were gone to UT-Martin, where my father had been offered another tenured faculty position. After all, in its December issue of that year, *Life* magazine named Martin one of the nine happy towns left in America, a fact the place still trumpets in its Chamber of Commerce pamphlets.

But Cary Medlin's murder seems now only the first in a series of violent crimes that punctuated my childhood, as though that early experience had magnetized us and others began to collect like iron filings. In 1983, four-year-old Marlena Childress disappeared from her front yard in the neighboring town of Union City, Tennessee (or so her mother Pamela Bailey said initially), last seen wearing a purple shirt and pants and jelly sandals. Marlena was the niece of my classmate Kristi Childress, a sweet girl and Martin Junior High cheerleader whose boyfriend in those years was a Meek Streeter named John Willoughby. (Age-progressed images suggesting what Marlena might look like now bear a remarkable resemblance to Kristi).

A search team numbering in the hundreds sought the girl for days until her mother confessed to authorities that she had accidentally struck and killed the girl and then dumped her body. Police dragged the Obion River but found nothing. Pamela Bailey changed her story again shortly thereafter: she hadn't killed her daughter after all. I remember wild speculation at the time about Marlena's whereabouts, including the theory that Bailey had sold her daughter for drugs. The case was profiled on Robert Stack's popular NBC series "Unsolved Mysteries," but no arrests were ever made in the case, no charges ever filed. Kristi Childress was in my homeroom the following year, our first at Westview High School, and I can recall our classmates inquiring, as tactfully as freshmen can, about her brother's little girl. After a while, we just stopped asking.

Then in January of 1985, another Meek Streeter, Harold "Mohawk" Powell, was arrested for the murder of a 24-year-old college student at the man's apartment near the Tennessee-Martin campus. My older sister Mary was in the Westview High cafeteria the day Martin police officers came to the school to arrest Harold, saw them carry hog-tied, grinning Powell out of first period lunch, through the front doors, and then dump him headfirst into the backseat of a police cruiser, and she told us all about it at the dinner table when she got home.

Harold had grown up in Jackson, Michigan, but moved to Tennessee when Goodyear closed the Jackson plant where Harold's father worked as a tire-builder ("Move to work at the Union City plant," Goodyear told its Jackson employees, "or go hungry."). He had curly red hair he often shaved into a namesake Mohawk and was, according to then Martin Police Chief Jackie Moore, an "exercise enthusiast" often observed running or biking through town. I remember watching him do pull-ups from chain link nets at the elementary school's basketball courts down the street from my house, biting his tongue against the strain, his head reddening with blood as the muscles in his back fanned like a cobra's hood. He and his brothers Scott and Ronnie lived just across the railroad tracks from Meek Street and frequented the basketball courts. As the bookish professor's kid, I took my share of ribbing from the Powells at the playground, though in larger contexts— at the city pool or ballgames— they seemed to show me a strange kind of Meek Street loyalty.

According to police, Powell bludgeoned music major William Crawford Henson with a length of steel pipe like that used for barbells and left the boy to die in his apartment, where Martin Police Sergeant Don Smothers found the body eight days later. Police also claimed Powell used Henson's 1981 Camaro as a temporary getaway car (the abandoned Camaro was the M.P.D.'s first sign something was amiss) and that he returned to steal clothing from the apartment days after the murder, clothing later found in Powell's home.

In October of that year, just as the first-degree murder trial was to get underway, Powell pled guilty to the lesser charge of second-degree murder and was sentenced to thirty years in state prison. District Attorney David Hayes (prosecutor in the Coe case) accepted the plea but still wondered about motive. "There's just no explanation," he told the court. Hayes did note that Powell's defense attorney would have argued the attack was provoked by Henson's homosexual advances toward the defendant, and that the plea bargain spared the Henson family a five-day trial that would have certainly involved demeaning allegations about their only son. "We deny that there were any advances," Hayes told reporters.

The last time I saw Harold Powell was when my American government class took a field trip to the Northwest Tennessee Regional Correctional Facility in Tiptonville, where my father sometimes taught extension courses for extra money during my junior year of high school. Harold stood under a backboard in the prison gymnasium rebounding basketballs. "Hey Bobby Cowser," Powell had called out. I was the only field tripper to get such a shout out from an inmate.

I called the prison recently to acquire about Powell, a little suspicious of the memory. Had he even served time there, I asked a woman there, and what about during my junior year? Yes, she told me, Powell had been at Tiptonville in 1986, paroled and on the streets after serving less than six years.

And these were merely the headlines. There were other violences— the domestic sort young Robert Glen Coe and his siblings endured, the suicide of my brother's grade school friend, the implication of another friend in the murder of a high school girl at a party in a neighboring town, corporal punishment in local schools. Not to mention what RFK once called the violence of institutions— inaction and ignorance, poverty and prejudice— which lay beneath what I observed.

James Hall's "Without Sanctuary" exhibition, a collection of lynching photos from early twentieth-century America, brought it all home to me, or me home to it, ten years after I'd first moved away: in particular, a photo of the 1902 lynching of Garfield Burley and Curtis Brown, two black men accused of shooting a young white farmer in the tiny Dyer County town of Newbern, forty miles from my home, where I used to catch the Amtrak train to New Orleans at the start of each college semester. The men represented two of the more than twenty men lynched in and around Weakley County, Tennessee, since the Civil War. I remember standing in a Burlington, Vermont, bookstore holding a copy of the issue of *PHOTO* magazine in which the photo appeared, recognizing Newbern landmarks in the background despite the dusty streets and the two men dangling from a telephone pole in the foreground. The photo confirmed something in me, far away as I was from home, like when I'd first seen that photo of searchers hunting Cary's Medlin's body: the sort of baseline brutality of the place I'd come from.

I left Martin for New Orleans, a city that was at the time (1988-1992) the nation's murder capital, averaging almost one slaying per day, then moved to Milwaukee to begin a master's program just in time to witness the demolition of Jeffrey Dahmer's Oxford Apartments on 25th Street, only a dozen blocks or so from the efficiency I was renting. So maybe there's nowhere to run from violence in America anyway. I spent a night in Toronto several years ago and happened to turn the channel to local coverage of a shooting at a downtown donut shop. "Geez, this isn't the States," an exasperated bystander told the reporter.

And of course I told and retold precisely my most grisly Tennessee stories to new acquaintances during those first get-to-know-me weeks of college, still retell them in classrooms now. Flannery O'Connor groused that their grotesqueries are the only fare most Northerners will accept as realistically Southern, first of all. And they are a manifestation of the deep ambivalence I still feel about the place. (See Quentin Compson in *Absalom* saying of the South, "I don't hate it, I don't…"). My mother, a through and through Northerner, blames all the ugliness on that little Godforsaken patch of Earth my father dragged us to, considers the family's move south terribly fateful, and I expect I left there feeling the way she did, though after I had been gone a while I could see a good deal of the ugliness as human nature regardless of locale (Emile Zola's "Nothing human disgusts me" has since become a kind of credo). And I have even found my way to loving some of the place the way I think my father and brother do. The voices in the Coe trial transcript, for instance, preserved so perfectly by the court reporter, bless her heart— well, I felt oddly at home reading those pages, despite everything terrible in the world happening therein.

*

If Coe's had been an Old South crime, something out of Faulkner or O'Connor or Erskine Caldwell, what O'Connor called "The School of Southern Degeneracy," and if he'd been victimized in the 1970s by "the great liberal mistake" of deinstitutionalization, then the 1990s saw him headed inevitably toward a New South punishment, caught in what Sister Helen Prejean called "the iron protocol of retributive justice" so in vogue in the 1990s among law-and-order politicians and prosecutors. "That's the way a machine works," wrote Prejean in a scathing appraisal of George W. Bush's refusal to grant clemency while Governor of Texas (of the 153 cases that came before Bush and his Attorney General Alberto Gonzalez, Bush intervened in only one, sending the other 152 men to their deaths). "Relentless and preordained," she wrote, "with no room for the personal transcendence that conscience gives... all so mechanical, so unthinking, so *political*."

In the 1960s, when civil rights were at the forefront of American civic consciousness, when Attorney General Robert Kennedy closed an inhumane Alcatraz and he and his brother had the country imagining a "Great Society" (a notion which likely led to the aforementioned "liberal mistake"), support for a death penalty was at an all-time low. The 1972 Furman v. Georgia Supreme Court decision effectively suspended capital punishment in America, and though the 1976 Gregg v. Georgia decision reinstated the death penalty (Gary Gilmour, subject of Norman Mailer's *Executioner's Song,* was famously the first man executed after reinstatement), in most states death chambers had been dormant for decades.

But the pendulum had begun to swing back in the 1980s and 90s, as Americans enjoyed/endured twelve consecutive years of Republican executive administration. Cornel West has called the period between Ronald Reagan's election in 1980 and the end of the second George W. Bush's eight years in office an "ice age" of moral concern, when it was fashionable to be indifferent to the suffering of the most vulnerable. As a backlash against perceived '70s leniency, we got tough on crime and today incarcerate more than 1 in 100 of our citizens, the highest rate of any nation in human history. While only 130 men were executed in the United States between 1977 and 1990, more than 1030 men have been put to death since 1990, a vast majority of these death sentences having been carried out in southern states where studies reveal citizens hold fast to a biblical belief in vengeance and retribution. Clifton Sain, a Christian studies major at Union University in Jackson, Tennessee, told a *Jackson Sun* reporter he believed only an ordained, God-fearing public official ought to make decisions about capital punishment. "If there is a chance that he's innocent, Christ will give him the answer." God-fearing public officials in Alabama, Arkansas, Georgia, South Carolina, Florida, and Oklahoma put dozens of men to death during this time.

Virginia executed nearly one hundred, and Texas more than 250.

In the '90s, legislators, southern lawmakers in particular, made campaign vows to rid their crowded prisons of the scores of the condemned men languishing there for decades while they exhausted their appeals (Bureau of Justice statistics had revealed that the average death row inmate had been spending 15-20 years waiting to be executed), undertaking, among other projects, a streamlining of *habeas corpus* legislation, a foundation of Anglo-American law for 300 years. In 1997 Harold McQueen became the first person executed in Kentucky in 35 years, and Coe was slated to be the first man put to death in neighboring Tennessee since 1960, the first ever by lethal injection.

Just as I arrived in Lincoln, Nebraska, in 1994 to begin Ph.D. studies there, the state was gearing up for its first execution since 1959 when Charlie Starkweather, nineteen-year-old murderer of eleven and inspiration for the Martin Sheen/ Sissy Spacek film "Badlands," had been put to death. The state planned to put to death Harold Lamont "Wili" Otey for the June 1977 murder of an Omaha woman named Jane McManus, and the case dominated local headlines and news broadcasts and was the talk of the English department where I was a new graduate assistant. Two women on the department faculty had helped form Nebraskans Against the Death Penalty, a grassroots group that opposed Otey's execution and the several slated to follow it. One of those women taught the orientation for new teaching assistants in which I was required to enroll, and though she never mentioned the execution in class, I heard her discussing it with students and colleagues in the hallways before and after class every day.

That's all the case was to me, a conversation in another room, only half-perceived. I was at the height of a period of single-minded self-regard then, something America seems to sanction in young people just making their way. I was beginning doctoral studies and was to be married at the end of that first semester, and I could not imagine Wili Otey's life and death had anything to do with mine.

Walking home from a night of drinking in Omaha, Otey had seen 26-year-old McManus through a window, asleep on her living room sofa. According to a confession the illiterate Otey later recanted, he entered the home through the back door intending only to steal the woman's stereo, but, waking her in the process, raped her as well. Otey, then 25, reported that the victim ultimately pleaded with him to kill her, and he obliged, striking her several times in the head with a hammer and strangling her with a belt.

He was to be put to death at 12:01 a.m. on a September Friday, the state hoping the odd hour would discourage crowds. After preparing the next day's classes the Thursday night before, I settled in to watch television. My fiancé was still living in Milwaukee and was not to join me in Lincoln until after the December wedding, so I was alone in that half-furnished 8th floor apartment most of the time, and it was not uncommon for me to stay up very late watching old movies or sitcom reruns, waiting to hear the melancholy "Taxi" theme at 2 a.m. before wandering back to the bedroom.

Local affiliates began to interrupt regular programming just after 10 p.m. to initiate a final Otey countdown. Special coverage included interviews with the victim's family, Otey's family, nuns from Kansas who had befriended Wili, attorneys for both sides, law enforcement officers involved with the case; file footage from the twenty-year-old Otey trial, and from the Starkweather case and execution thirty-five years before; tours of the penitentiary, death row, and the chamber housing the electric chair. All of this and periodic live remote broadcasts from the parking lot of the prison, which I had happened to spy one afternoon while jogging, out across the state highway which belted the city, the barb-wired prison compound the only landmark on what was otherwise lonely prairie.

What I saw on the television suggested the late hour had not discouraged crowds— there were throngs pro and con, hundreds strong. It is a great irony, Foucault points out in *Discipline and Punish*, that the public should be so drawn "to a spectacle intended to terrorize it." The group protesting the execution had an air of solemnity at first— praying, singing hymns, bearing candles. A vigil. Leaders exhorted them to ignore the pro-execution faction beginning to assemble just across police barricades. "Folks, do you want *them* to be the focus of attention?" one leader yelled, "Just ignore these barbarians."

Ultimately, though, they began to respond to the jeers of the other mob— mostly young men, mostly drunk— whose assembly resembled the bonfire pep rally before the homecoming game. Public execution has carried with it, Foucault reminds, from the time when the accused was put to death before the eyes of the jeering multitudes, "a whole aspect of the carnivalesque, in which rules were inverted, authorities mocked." After trading insults a while, the crowds began to push against each other.

I could not avert my eyes, watched every moment of

the broadcast. For all my proximity to violence, I had never before lived in a state capital so close to state-sponsored executions. Moreover I was a Nebraskan now, albeit a newly-minted one, my teaching assistant stipend the equivalent of the state dole when you got down to it, and the sentence to be carried out only miles from where I sat that night, out at the edge of the good and easy life I imagined for myself, and it would be carried out in my name. The State of Nebraska versus Wili Otey. That weighed heavily on me.

The execution sequence began at 12:23 a.m. and Otey was pronounced dead just ten minutes later. All local stations went to their on-scene reporters for the official pronouncement, and a roar rose from the pro-death penalty carnival. State-appointed media witnesses met for a news conference shortly thereafter. "My opinion has changed on this matter," I remember one middle-aged Omaha reporter saying, visibly shaken. The camera panned the cheering crowd outside; I thought I saw Randy Borg from my 9:30 class bodysurfing atop the arms of the other revelers in his trademark Orlando Magic ball cap.

Borg was like most of the young men I taught in my four years in Lincoln (we were warned in orientation that our classes would be remarkably homogenous, in appearance and attitude). Raised in one of the small cities that sprang up along Interstate 80 between Lincoln and Scottsbluff, a town like Fremont or Grand Island or Kearney, blue-eyed, blonde-headed Randy Borg had come to the university as a matter of course, the next thing to do, certain that the good life was his birthright and the rest was gravy. A first-generation college student, if I remember right, he was pleasant and polite in class but not much persuaded that my first-year composition class had anything to offer him. Maybe he was right. Thin and tall, Randy sat in the back of the basement classroom in Andrews Hall where our class met, slouched so his bony knees were level with his shoulders, the Orlando Magic cap pulled low over his eyes.

I did not sleep well that night. Mostly, I hoped it had not been Randy I'd seen on the television. Perhaps identifying him there finally connected my life to Otey's; I was awakening to the fact that Nebraska's electric chair, as U.S. Poet Laureate Ted Kooser wrote in a poem later, now sat "in each Nebraskan's home… part of our dark oppressive furniture."

But any hope I had of being mistaken about Randy was gone as soon as I saw him the next morning in class, wearing the ball cap and the clothes he'd had on the night before, looking like he had come to class straight from the prison. He sat in the middle of the room surrounded by male classmates, regaling them with stories. "I heard his skin bubbled where they strapped him in," one said. Randy could not confirm it.

I did not know how to proceed— not the first time that semester. Our mentors in Nebraska's composition program encouraged us to have students write from their own lives and discouraged broaching the typically polarizing social issues— abortion, gun control, euthanasia, capital punishment— which I had been asked to write about in the composition course I'd taken as a freshman, "The Analysis of Argument." I did not want to step out of bounds.

"I saw you on television last night," I finally said to him.

"Yeah?" he said.

"Whether or not you think the guy deserved it," I said,

"didn't it strike you as a solemn occasion?"

"That's just the media making you feel that way," Randy said.

What *does* make me feel the way I do? Sociologists P.D. Ellsworth and S.R. Gross suggest Americans' views on issues like the death penalty tend not to be entirely rational, that people who oppose capital punishment, for example, would continue to do so even if it proved to be an effective deterrent to crime, and that people who support it would continue to do so even though they are aware of racial and economic inequities and the rank capriciousness of its administration. I have this "boxers or briefs" theory that we grow either as little prosecutors or little public defenders, sympathizing with one side or the other in such situations, and that this predisposition has a powerful effect on our thinking as adults.

But where does even that begin? When Albert Camus was a small boy, his father had been eager to attend the execution, by guillotine, of a man convicted of the murder of a local farm family, but when his father returned home, he fell to the floor and vomited at what he'd seen. The event became for Camus the cornerstone of his long and principled objection to capital punishment. Did I experience such an adumbration? Was my predisposition a product of what I witnessed as a child?

In high school I am afraid I swallowed whole a load of coachspeak and clung to a child's absolute understanding of fairness and justice (do the crime and do the time, etc.). Like Randy Borg, I guess, I had thought equivocation and mitigation were for losers. In an A.P. English debate in my senior year, my football teammates and I argued the position that Macbeth was more of a man than wimpy, indecisive

Hamlet (we wore, at my insistence, blue sport coats and neckties to the competition).

Mostly I was just a naif. I had arrived in New Orleans amid the 1988 Republican convention completely oblivious to the meeting's purpose or significance and told anyone who asked that I was "apolitical." I was busy ruining myself with poems and did not see the point of political engagement (though three successive Republican administrations in my adolescence no doubt contributed to this disaffection). I don't even think my attitude was all that unusual for the time; I can remember a hallmate in my freshman dorm, a finance major, who idolized Gordon Gecko from the Oliver Stone movie "Wall Street" and wore paisley suspenders as an expression of this devotion.

But one of the first essays I wrote for an interpretive journalism class during my sophomore year was about a high school teammate of mine— a kid from Meek Street whose front door was visible from our back door— who'd garnered many Division I scholarship offers in football and baseball but who'd had to rely on my mother's help to finish his junior and senior English term papers and who, after a full year of passing grades in remedial courses at a local junior college, still hadn't earned a single college credit. In my essay, I referred to Dan Quayle's famous '88 campaign anecdote about his grandmother telling him "You can do anything you want if you just set your mind to it and go to work," and offered my friend's story as counterpoint. "I wish he was smart like Bobby," my friend's mother had told my parents when she'd come over to thank them for the study help, but it was about more than smarts, and we all knew it.

Chapter 9:
Avenging Angel

Whenever any American's life is taken by another American unnecessarily— whether it is done in the name of the law or in the defiance of the law, by one man or a gang, in cold blood or in passion, in an attack of violence or in response to violence... whenever we tear at the fabric of life... the whole nation is degraded.

Robert F. Kennedy, "On the Mindless Menace of Violence" Delivered at the City Club of Cleveland (Cleveland, Ohio, April 5, 1968)

Robert Glen Coe developed a nasty reputation with the Tennessee Department of Corrections during his early time as its ward, regularly spitting at prison staff and masturbating in his cell in plain view of guards and other inmates. Warden Ricky Bell confirmed in court documents Coe's suspicion that, because of the nature of his crime, most of his fellow inmates wanted to kill him. With little hope that his conviction might be overturned, Coe's sisters say he withdrew, from family and friends and attorneys, participating half-heartedly at best in legal efforts.

People who worked to save Coe's life could not help but think of him as a frightened little boy, prone to petulance and sullenness. Underneath the vulgarity, they said, lay terrific fear. He had begun his incarceration at the old Tennessee State Penitentiary outside Nashville, built in 1898 in the style of the famous Auburn, New York, prison (birthplace of striped prisoner uniforms and nighttime lockdown). But the old state pen was now defunct and, like the Shelby County Courthouse, the location for many movies and television shows, including *The Glass Castle* and *The Green Mile*. Perpetually overcrowded (1,400 inmates were processed into the 800-bed facility the day it opened in 1898), conditions on the old Death Row were declared unconstitutionally bad in 1982 and rioting inmates did thousands of dollars of damage in the summer of 1985, so that Tennessee was compelled to construct a new state maximum security facility, the Riverbend complex on the Cumberland River, and in 1989 Tennessee's Death Row was relocated there.

In a handwritten letter sent in August of 1982 from his Death Row cell, a desperate but respectful Robert Coe professes his innocence and pleads with the Tennessee Supreme Court for another hearing. He writes in his neat, middle-school cursive that his new attorney, Walker Quinn, has filed appeals which "do not meet my approval," that he'd like to fire Quinn but Judge Williams won't allow him. "If you'll [sic] can't see the wrongfulness of my being here and give me a new trial," the letter goes on, "then please, I beg you to leave my case as it is. Because I don't want to live in a world that is so unjust." Coe denied that he was insane, "a sick or crazy man," despite claims made by his attorney. "The only problem I have at this time is being locked up and having him as my lawyer," he writes.

But when in 1983 the state supreme court upheld the original jury's 1981 conviction, dismissing Coe's allegations that jury selection was mishandled and the prosecution's playing his taped confession in open court inflamed jurors (something the court called "improper" but "harmless"), a despondent Coe fired off another missive, dated the 4th of July, this one expletive-filled and increasingly angry. "I have lost all feeling for how you so-called people hand out justice," the second letter begins. "I have lost all respect for you'll [sic]. I do not wish to appeal to a higher court. As I told you before, either give me freedom or murder me," he continues. "Your decision was wrong in my case," writes a petulant Coe, "but I don't guess it bothers you people any." He explains he has no interest in further appeals, citing again an unjust world not fit to live in. "Now I can see why our country is in trouble," Coe says in closing, "because it's ran by a bunch of dick sucking [sic] bastards like you people in the Tenn. Supreme Court! So fuck each of you in your ass!"

In August of 1984, Coe made the first of several Death Row suicide attempts, swallowing thirty mild sedatives prescribed by prison doctors to help him sleep (he was taking more than thirty different medications daily at the time of his execution in 2000). A fellow inmate discovered him unconscious at 7 a.m. the morning following the ingestion and guards removed him to the infirmary where he awakened hours later. Coe had left behind a suicide note, handwritten on legal paper like the letters to the Supreme Court, blasting "inhumane" prison conditions and then-warden Michael Dutton. "I am not ashamed of a single thing that I've done," Coe's note read, "I only wish I had done more."

Newspapers declared much of the rest of the letter "unprintable," including an obscene cartoon Coe added at the bottom of the page. Earlier in that year, the United States Court of Appeals had also refused to hear Coe's case, denying him a *writ of certiorari*, and the *Weakley County Press* reported Coe had ordered counsel, now provided by the

Southern Prison Ministry, to cease further legal action on his behalf. In the note, Coe warned against destroying the letter, claiming to have mailed copies to acquaintances outside the prison, and willed personal belongings, a fan and a television, to his mother. District Attorney David Hayes, the second-hand source of most of the note's content, was upset by Coe's attempt to "control his own destiny" and deprive the state of the opportunity to take his life.

Coe was reaching the end of the allotted two decades the average inmate spends on Death Row, and folks in and around Greenfield shared the growing national irritation with what seemed like the endless appeals process in capital cases. Union City *Daily Messenger* reporter John Brannon filed a special report in the *Weakley County Press* detailing the thousands of dollars taxpayers had spent on Coe's incarceration and appeals, including the names of the sixteen attorneys who had represented him in state and federal proceedings. Which is not to mention, Brannon writes, the paralegals, private investigators, and expert witnesses employed in Coe's defense and paid with taxpayer money. "How many appeals does a guy get?" longtime Greenfielder James Roy Pope wondered in *The Jackson Sun*. Former investigator Jack Blackwell told the paper he understood the process, but it still frustrated him: "It really don't make no sense to keep this thing batted back and forth, back and forth, back and forth, with this thing happening Labor Day weekend, 1979. It just needs to be settled. I think something needs to be done to bring this thing to a close."

*

Charlotte Stout had expressed relief at the time of

Robert Glen Coe's 1979 arrest that he would cause no other parent the grief she was experiencing, but she seemed uninterested in what came next for her daughter's killer, saying no punishment would bring Cary Ann back anyway. Yet by the time of the 1981 trial, the girl's mother was testy on the witness stand, eager to see justice done and frustrated by those she thought stood in its way.

She says she would have preferred to stay out of the limelight altogether, like Cary's father, who granted nary an interview and returned to Tennessee from Florida for important court proceedings but by no means all of them. "I'm a just country girl and a nurse," Mrs. Stout told a U.S. House of Representatives subcommittee in 1997. Only her father-in-law Joe William Stout, Cary's step-grandfather, made that impossible, taking it upon himself to serve as family spokesperson in the days after the murder, though he could hardly be said to have known the little girl very well. Charlotte Stout wanted to correct all Joe's misinformation and felt it her duty to keep her daughter's memory alive.

By the time I had begun to think again about the case in the middle '90s, Mrs. Stout had become an all-out crusader for Coe's execution, a media darling always at the ready with a sound byte or a dig for her opponents, consenting to dozens of interviews, national and local, print and broadcast, honored by the *Weakley County Press* one Mother's Day for her courage in the face of tragedy and determination to remain positive despite it.

Charlotte and Mickey Stout had made every attempt to resume their lives after Cary's murder. Charlotte gave birth to Joshua Lance Stout weeks after Cary's murder, and to Mickey's third son, Jesse McKinley Stout, their second together, a few years later (My father had one of the boys in a composition class at the university. Joshua, he thinks.). Charlotte continued to work as a nurse, rising in time to the position of nurse auditor, a "clinical review/reimbursement specialist" with Blue Cross/ Blue Shield of Tennessee. But her reality had been changed forever, she told me by phone in 2006: "Everything that was good in me had been drained."

Mickey Stout eventually left Goodyear to begin his own career in medicine, moving the family fifty miles south to Jackson for a change of scenery and so he could begin working as a med tech at the Jackson-Madison County Hospital. But the Stouts missed home and moved back a decade later. Charlotte seemed to have emerged from grief's fog in that time, and her pain came into sharper focus. "I realized the whole world did not do this to me," she told me, "Robert Coe did."

And just in time, since Coe's appeals, after more than a decade of futility, were beginning to find purchase. Through the 1980s, state and federal courts had refused Coe's numerous petitions, but in 1992 Coe's attorneys filed a second *habeas corpus* petition, this time in the Federal Supreme Court, Middle Tennessee District, Judge John T. Nixon presiding, and Nixon agreed to consider the case. Nixon's critics claim Tennessee's Death Row defendants, free to choose the district in which their appeals would be heard, invariably chose Nixon's district, where no death sentence had been upheld since President Jimmy Carter appointed him in 1980. And while more and more men were meeting their end in gas chambers and electric chairs around the South, Tennessee remained the only former confederate state that had not resumed executions since 1976— all thanks, said his detractors, to Judge Nixon.

John Trice Nixon had the truest of Southern pedigrees, grandson of two confederate soldiers, son of one of the original authors of the Agrarian manifesto *I'll Take My Stand* (his father, Vanderbilt political science professor Herman Clarence Nixon, penned the chapter "Whither Southern Economy"). Yet the family had a progressive streak too, his populist father often taking moral stands that were personally costly: an early critic of segregation accused of Communist associations during the red scare of the 1940s and '50s, H.C. Nixon had resigned from the faculty at Tulane early in his career and disagreed with fellow Agrarians on the matter of sensible industrialization and cooperative farming as means of alleviating rural southern poverty.

Young John Nixon took this example greatly to heart. After college at Harvard (a la Quentin Compson) and a stint in the Army in the late '50s, he returned to Nashville for law school at Vanderbilt, moving then into private practice near family roots in Alabama. But before long he found himself a Civil Rights attorney, spending months in Selma monitoring Martin Luther King's voting rights marches and working desegregation strategies for Mississippi school districts before returning to Tennessee and a state job in the early 1970s.

Judge Nixon has always been forthcoming regarding his position on the death penalty, making it plain in a rare interview with a *Nashville Scene* writer: it *is* possible to administer it fairly and without violating the defendant's 8th amendment rights (the Supreme Court's concern in the 1972 Furman v. Georgia decision), except procedural mistakes are often made in capital cases and, since there's no going back once the switch has been flipped or the syringe inserted, it is the responsibility of a federal judge to review each case meticulously and identify any such errors, vacating sentences in those instances and granting condemned prisoners new trials. After states like Tennessee changed death penalty laws in response to the Supreme Court's Furman criticism, Nixon felt, with rules about jury instruction so new (1978 in Tennessee's case), mistakes in cases heard in those first few years were only to be expected.

In any event, Nixon contends, the death penalty ought to be the weapon of last resort in a community's crime-fighting arsenal, like nuclear weapons in a military stockpile (research is with Nixon here, suggesting Americans' support for the capital punishment is a "mile wide but an inch deep," most people favoring life without parole to actual execution when offered the choice). It's not inconsistent, Nixon says, for a community to have capital punishment on the books and yet use it with extreme caution and grave reluctance. He learned to live with contradiction from a father who loved his Southern heritage yet lobbied to make any change he thought would help his fellow man.

Nixon's 1992 decision even to hear the Robert Glen Coe case made him a lightning rod for criticism. In Greenfield, Cary Ann's elementary school principal, Richard Wade, headed up the movement "Impeach Judge Nixon" (Charlotte Stout was named to the board of directors, though she later claimed not to be an official member, merely "officially associated because of her concerns"), collecting more than 27,000 signatures from small-town Tennesseans wondering whatever happened to justice. Nixon had vacated death penalty convictions in four other cases, technicalities all according to Wade, and in most cases higher courts had affirmed his rulings.

It took Nixon four years to rule (another complaint of the impeachment mob), but following an April 1996 hearing Nixon did vacate Coe's convictions that December, on the grounds that original Judge William Williams did not give the jury enough guidance when he defined the terms "heinous, atrocious and cruel," "reasonable doubt" and "malice." Nixon's ruling did not put Coe on the street, only back into the courtroom, before another judge. But Charlotte Stout could hardly endure the thought of another trial, all the memories that would conjure, the evidence now almost twenty years old and lead investigator Alvin Daniel dead. TBI inspector Jack Blackwell even suggested Daniel's death had spurred the *habeas* filing, Coe's defense attorneys hoping incriminating evidence had been lost or forgotten. Impeach Judge Nixon members demonstrated in Nashville city parks, news media lambasted the judge— this must be what brought the case back onto my radar out in Nebraska, following as it did on the heels of the Otey execution: the public outcry against Nixon.

In 1997, Charlotte Stout accompanied her state representative John Tanner (D, Union City) to Washington where she spoke before the Judiciary Committee of the U.S. House of Representatives on the issue of judicial misconduct and "activist judges." "I'm not here today as an avenging mother," she told the assembled representatives, who included John Conyers, Barney Frank, and the late Sonny Bono. "I will not go into lengthy details about our case," she read from a prepared statement, "lest you think I am an angry mother with a heart set on revenge." She merely represented, she said, the more than 27,000 "blue collar" Tennesseans frustrated by Nixon's interference with the wheels of justice who feared he would overturn every capital conviction that came before him if allowed to continue down this "historical path."

Poster mother for this frustration was not a role she relished, she told the committee, simple country girl that she was, but Nixon had to go— the delays, the placing of personal conscience before the law, accepting awards from an anti-death penalty clergy organization and other such conflicts of interest. The Supreme Court has deemed the death penalty constitutional, she reminded lawmakers. "It shouldn't even be an issue. I didn't know [Coe] was going before a judge infamous for overturning death penalty cases," she said. "Nobody told me I had the right to be there. If a judge turns over a conviction and sentence for the man who killed my daughter, I want him to look me in the face and tell me why. What a tragedy if a federal judge is allowed flagrant misconduct in office and our elected representatives refuse to discipline him," said Stout, "for the sake of protecting the independence of the judiciary. Since the reinstatement of capital punishment in 1977 in the state of Tennessee," Stout told the committee, "there has not been one execution."

As America got tough on crime, the Victim's Rights movement was taking hold nationally as well. Marcia Clark and the other O.J. Simpson prosecutors had taken heat for wearing angel pins in solidarity with victims Ron Goldman and Nicole Brown Simpson, and I understood the criticism: prosecutors acted on behalf of the state, after all, not victims and families. I remember watching grief-crazed survivors scream at Jeffrey Dahmer during "victim impact statements" during the sentencing phase of his trial and thinking that the whole circus was beneath dignity. But though American courts traditionally had been sensitive to defense attorneys' claims that the presence of the victim's family at trial could unduly influence juries, high-profile trials like Simpson's and Dahmer's had begun to effect widespread change. Crime victims' families became celebrities, interviewed by Geraldo and Oprah. Charlotte Stout was the face of victims' rights in Tennessee, working to streamline *habeas* provisions in Tennessee and to enact a bill that would guarantee the rights of crime victims and their families.

*

It was public outcry that brought me back to the Coe case, via the news clippings my parents began to send out to me in Nebraska and the stories I found on the Internet, but it was Charlotte Stout who held my attention.

Despite the empty things people tell the grieving at funerals— that "there are no words," that we "can't imagine"— one can try to imagine suffering a loss like Charlotte Stout's. In fact, I believe it's the first thing we do— try to imagine, as long as we can stand it. Sometimes imagination provides the only route to sympathy. "What if it was your son?" is the question always placed before someone inclined toward mercy for the accused in a case like this, after all. I believe there is a sense in which the community was so awed by the magnitude of Charlotte Stout's loss that it abdicated all responsibility for the disposition of the matter— give the poor lady whatever she wants, so to speak.

I think about how fierce my own mother was in my defense when I was a boy, how I relied on that grizzly-sow ferocity growing up, how many times it saved me. And how quick to anger I can be when I perceive that either of my own boys has been wronged. "I'd kill for my children," is the kind of thing I hear mothers and fathers say as though it were the most profound expression of parental love.

Still, if we're lucky, we'll only ever need to imagine the grief and rage Charlotte Stout must have felt and perhaps still feels, and the difficulty for me lies in generating that kind of ferocity on behalf of someone else's child, by proxy. Canadian political scientist and capital punishment proponent Walter Berns wrote in the seventies, at the height of America's death penalty debate, that criminals are rightly the objects of our anger, that our communal anger is an expression of our caring for one another, that our anger becomes generous when it protects the community by demanding that transgressors be punished (Foucault says capital punishment is the means by which the community can inscribe its grief and rage on the body of the transgressor). I have simply never been able to summon such communal anger. I see disease and pathos in the Medlin murder but not evil, and believe responsibility in the case may apply more broadly than is popularly acknowledged.

I wrote a short letter to Charlotte Stout in 2006, announcing myself as Cary's classmate and explaining that I planned to be in Tennessee that fall to read the transcripts and conduct interviews and that I hoped that we could at least sit down and talk. It has occurred to me only lately how this book is, among other things, an attempt to wrest the story from the woman who's clutched it for nearly thirty years. I sensed I needed Charlotte's help to tell my version of the story, for fairness' sake and for all she knows about her daughter that I never will. I'm hardly the ideal audience for her version, yet I would have dearly loved to read the short biography Charlotte Stout says she's written about Cary's life, titled "Cary's Legacy," which she conceived as a keepsake for the younger brothers and nieces and nephews Cary Ann never had the chance to meet. I remember some film I once saw of Anne Frank, found on an Amsterdam neighbor's reel-to-reel home video fifty years after her death, little Anne waving from a high window along the Merwedeplein, and how it stilled my heart to see it. I imagine Charlotte Stout's manuscript might hold the same shiver.

But Charlotte Stout cancelled our face-to-face once I'd arrived in town— all her chronic conditions flaring up, she said, Krohn's disease and systemic lupus— so I had to call her from my parents' house, on the phone in my sisters' old bedroom. Right away, she asked about how I felt about the death penalty. If I had been a little disingenuous in my original letter, I thought here I needed to be straight. I think it shames us all, I said, borrowing a line from the Memphis writer Beverly Lowry. There was a change in Charlotte's voice thereafter; she handled me the way she'd handled Coe's attorney during his cross examination of her, and I'm afraid she gave me exactly what she had given every other reporter over the last three decades. I had read it all in other interviews.

"What were you serving for dinner that night?" I asked her toward the end of the conversation.

"Oh, lasagna," she told me. "Ever-body knows that. Told that to many reporters. Haven't done as much research as you think you have."

Chapter 10:
Sympathy for the Devil

> Do not say, "Yes, but these are isolated, peripheral examples. These are marginal Americans, uneducated. They tell us nothing about ourselves." They tell us everything about ourselves. And even the telling, the exposure, is a kind of cutting, an inscription in the flesh.
>
> Joyce Carol Oates, "They All Just Went Away"

Tennessee Attorney General Paul Summers appealed Nixon's reversal of the Coe conviction to the Sixth Circuit Court of Appeals in Cincinnati and on November 16, 1996, the three-judge panel sided with Summers and the state, reinstating Coe's conviction and death sentence. Then in March of 1999, that same Circuit Court refused Coe's petition to have his case reviewed by the full panel of judges, making his approaching execution date of October 19, 1999, suddenly seem very real. By May of 1999 Coe was once again under an order of execution, and in late September Warden Ricky Bell visited Coe to inform him of his right to choose the means by which he'd be executed, electrocution or lethal injection. If he did not choose, Bell explained, he'd die in the state's oak-paneled electric chair, "Old Sparky" as it was known. Coe signed an affidavit choosing lethal injection.

Coe would be the first to be executed in such a manner

in Tennessee, William Tines having been electrocuted back on November 7, 1960. Tines's execution, pushed from the front pages by Nashville and Memphis newspapers by JFK election coverage, has been called a "legal lynching" by death penalty abolitionists: a black man, called "boy" by his own attorney, put to death for the rape of a middle-aged white widow who could not identify him in court, whose doctor could not confirm that she was even raped (she testified she woke up bloody and just "felt like" she'd been violated). Thirty-three-year-old Tines, an illiterate whose own father had died as an inmate at Tennessee's Brushy Mountain State Prison in 1937, had prior convictions for petty larceny and horse thievery and double murder (he killed two men in a downtown Knoxville gunfight) and was serving a life sentence at Brushy Mountain for the murder conviction. He was an escapee in 1957 at the time of the aggravated rape. Newly-elected Governor Ellington refused clemency to Tines, though he only months later commuted the death sentence of a white murderer to 99 years.

*

When former army major Glenn Pruden became Tennessee Assistant Attorney General and head of the state's death penalty team in 1994, he could not believe the disarray he found when the state's ten capital cases, including the Coe file, were handed over. Some had never been assigned to a state attorney. But Pruden was a firm believer in the justice system and in retribution as its key component, in its efficient, machine-like operation. He soon had his office in military order, consolidating all files in a sophisticated new database and assigning an attorney to every case. Pruden did not consider himself an introspective man and had no qualms about carrying out executions, which were to his mind the best means by which the state could show a victim's family that it cares. If Tennessee was to have its death penalty machine (Helen Prejean's term) up and running again, he knew organization and efficiency would be crucial.

But Pruden was also learning that without regular use even a death penalty machine falls into disrepair, like those cars on Meek Street resting on blocks, weeds poking through open hoods— the law of entropy. Nobody knew how to work the thing, for one— there was no procedure at all for lethal injection. Corrections officers would have to be recruited and trained. Other states that, like Tennessee, required civilian witnesses to executions were having trouble identifying willing candidates.

Media rhetoric serves as crucial catalyst to this death penalty machine: in the case of a twenty-year-old crime, even a child murder considered one of the most heinous in state history, the people need to be reminded why the state should carry out its ultimate punishment. And if the public's orientation to the death penalty, as studies suggest, is largely emotional and nonrational, then narrative— storytelling— would be the way to reach them. The state had to present the Cary Medlin story as prosecutor David Hayes had presented it in his closing argument back in 1979, sentimentally: Coe as a hungry shark "up from the bottom for another bite" (again, appropriated pop lyrics), Cary Medlin as idealized victim, not merely a beautiful nine-year-old girl robbed of her future but a girl who had lived eighty years in eight, saintly, idealized.

In "Sentimental Journeys," Joan Didion's brilliant essay

on the 1989 Central Park Jogger case, she writes that the victim in such cases is usually rendered in details stressing her "'difference,' or superior class," that this emphasis distorts and flattens the victim, "ultimately to suggest not the actual victim of an actual crime but a fictional character of a slightly earlier period...." In Cary's case, something out of a fairy tale. Little Red Riding Hood.

"Stories in which terrible crimes are inflicted on innocent victims," Didion continues, "offering as they do a... sentimental reading of the class differences and human suffering, a reading that promises both resolution and retribution, have long performed... as a built-in source of natural morphine working to blur the edges of real and to a great extent insoluble problems." This kind of narrative comforts us, says Didion, "with the assurance that the world is knowable." There are no larger social issues to be examined, in other words. Coe's poverty, domestic history and mental health are immaterial, not in the least mitigating. He is evil, the devil, the shark, the Big Bad Wolf, "The Misfit," and must be put an end to. You did not place him in the electric chair, Hayes told that original 1981 jury; he placed himself there. It's a simple matter of free will. All that testimony to the effect that Coe was not crazy, was a rational decision-maker who'd made a bad choice (the language used, incidentally, at my younger son's daycare center). "Don't worry your pretty little heads," was the message. "Let's get this over with."

Local reporters seemed complicit, abandoning traditional journalistic principles like objectivity in their coverage. As frustrated as Charlotte Stout at the molasses-slow appeals process, they too called for a swift end to the matter. John Brannon began a veritable one-man campaign for Coe's execution, publishing his "special reports" in the *Weakley County Press*. "Coe Should Already Be Dead" was the headline for an article Brannon filed in July of 1999 about public sentiment in Greenfield regarding Coe's punishment. "They wish someone had shot him the day they brought him in," Greenfield Dairy Queen proprietor Donna Bodkins told Brannon of her fellow Greenfielders. "If Coe doesn't deserve the electric chair," Bodkins's husband added, "there's nobody on the face of this Earth what does."

In the next piece in the series, "When Evil Wears a Human Face," Brannon recapped the case, skirting the details of Coe's confession, citing graphic language which "paints a word picture guaranteed to turn your stomach… things… most people would relate in reluctant whispers— things too perverse to cite in the pages of a family newspaper." Brannon calls it "incredible" that Coe's attorneys were still filing appeals, raising "issues" [emphasis Brannon's] regarding the original trial.

Editorial page commentary in the *Commercial Appeal* called Coe "vermin," decrying "exorbitant legal fees… to keep this animal alive." "Step on him as you would a cockroach," suggested one *Appeal* reader.

Characterizations of Coe in *The Jackson Sun* were worse: he was called a "freak of nature," a "rattlesnake," and a "monster." "Executing Coe," wrote an editor, "is no more than taking out the trash." "He is not human," opined one letter-writer, but "a crazed animal." Of course dehumanizing Coe, according to University of Memphis researchers Vandiver and Giocapassi, is a crucial element in the process of denying the Coe camp's claims to moral consideration (perhaps their last hope in the matter).

I remember one editorial in particular written by a *Weakley County Press* editor who was roughly my age but had not grown up in Martin and had not known Cary. She regularly wrote about working motherhood and her young children, about appreciating the simple things and focusing on what mattered. "She will never be forgotten," the editor wrote of Cary Ann, "by those who loved her and those who never got the chance to meet her." The illogic of her sentimental appropriation irked me— how could one miss what one had never known?

My students don't understand my crusade against sentimentality in their writing. "It's a lie," I tell them. "Sentimental narratives ask me to accept the world as greatly reduced, much less complex than the one we actually experience." I should have them read this book.

*

The defense had a narrative of its own, one in which Robert Glen Coe was an innocent man represented by hapless counsel at his original trial, railroaded by TBI and state's attorney officials who coerced a confession and destroyed exculpatory evidence.

Glenn Pruden considered defense motions for a stay guerilla tactics, prompted by the recent death of lead TBI investigator Alvin Daniel, but Coe's new defense team from the federal public defender's office was desperate.

There was no real hope for clemency. Though Illinois Governor George Ryan had declared a death penalty moratorium in that state in May of 2000, citing persistent problems in its administration (thirteen condemned men had been later exonerated in Ryan's state alone), Tennessee's

Republican Governor Donald Sundquist had said publically he thought Coe's alleged crime was a perfect argument for why the state ought to resume executions, that he was "outraged" the process of executing Coe had taken nearly twenty years. Experts thought that if Coe were in fact to be executed many more on the state's death row would follow soon after. Paul Bottei and Kelley Henry and Henry Martin knew they had to try to exonerate their client.

The team believed passionately in Coe's innocence. The dyed hair and bus ticket these supporters explained as the irrational behavior of a crazy man, the confession as the wild claims of said crazy man greatly frightened by investigators who, if you listened closely to the recording made in the county jail, did a great deal of coaching during that confession, particularly about the time that the crime had been committed. Look to Donald Gant, they said, who had a history of inappropriate sexual advances toward young girls and, unlike Coe, no alibi for the night of the murder. Explain the fresh scratch marks police found on his neck when he was questioned. What about the bloody sheets found at his home never given to Coe's original attorneys (and since "misplaced" at the TBI crime lab)? Gant admitted he was in Greenfield on September 1st and changed his story each time he was questioned. The key witnesses, Maggie and little Michael Stout and Herbert Clement, had identified Gant and not Coe in police line-ups in the days after the murder.

Furthermore, Coe's attorneys claimed, no physical evidence linked their client to the crime. Hair found on Cary Medlin's body did not match Robert Glen Coe. Though Agent Daniel claimed at trial that he could not match Coe's tire tread with any of the tracks found in the mud at Bean

Switch Road that afternoon in 1979 because the ambulance and search vehicles had compromised the crime scene, Coe's attorneys found tracks that matched Donald Gant's tire tread.

Coe's supporters came, by and large, from among the professionally compassionate— public defenders, the clergy, death penalty abolitionists, and so on— mobilized if not by particular regard for Robert or belief in his innocence than by the prospect of Coe's being put to death and what that would mean for Tennessee's future. Amnesty International appealed to Sundquist in an open letter, and singer/songwriter Steve Earle spoke on Coe's behalf at Nashville rallies.

My childhood friend Reverend Sky McCracken was the Methodist minister serving the Coe family in the last months of Robert's life. I've known Sky since he was a trumpeter in the high-school band that marched in front of my house and an umpire for the Little League at the ballpark across the street in the years that I worked there as a scorekeeper. His brother Vance took my older sister to the high school prom. Five years older than me, he remembers the day of Coe's arrest when, as a high-school freshman, he said in his gentle mother's hearing, "they should find a tree and hang the sonofabitch."

"Is that your Christian upbringing talking?" his mother asked him calmly.

McCracken says he carried the shame of that remark for twenty years, until the Memphis diocese announced Coe's family needed a pastor and he volunteered. As a member of the Weakley County Rescue Squad as a young man, he'd seen the crime scene photos and was horrified, knocked off his pins. But he'd been ordained as a minister in the meantime as well. "The service was my chance for redemption," he told me over lunch in the small western Kentucky town where he's now installed as pastor.

But public pro-death penalty sentiment was strong where the Coe/Medlin case was concerned. University of Memphis researchers Vandiver and Giocapassi joined peaceful protests every Wednesday for more than a year and a half on a busy Memphis street corner at rush hour, holding placards expressing their opposition to the death penalty and were amazed at the vitriol they were met with from passersby. "I hope your mother is killed by an axe murderer," one young man yelled from his car. "Pardon me?" said one protester, whereupon the young driver spat on him and drove away. Protesters were met daily with epithets, obscene gestures and bible verses. One woman glared at the demonstrators while she stuck her fingers down her throat.

*

On October 7, 1999, nine days before the scheduled execution, *The Jackson Sun* printed a letter Charlotte Stout had mailed to Coe on Death Row.

> Robert,
>
> I am sure you are being overwhelmed with letters from those opposed to capital punishment and from newspaper and other media reporters. You did say that killing Cary Ann would make you "famous" and ironically you are right. I think "infamous" is a better word.
>
> I have sent word to Warden Bell and to the Governor's office that if you wish to speak to me, I will come to Nashville to meet with you. You not only took

Cary's life that Saturday; you forever altered all your own family's lives and mine.

Stories in newspapers get altered and changed and do not always reflect truth. Your federal lawyers, in attempts to save your life, have tried to cast doubt in the public mind. The result has been lies, and more pain for our family, yours and everyone involved.

In 12 days you are scheduled to die. You have an exact date and time, which is more than most people know about their own death. You have the opportunity to make some of the most important decisions in your life.

I am a believer, as was Cary, in an all-powerful, eternal God. I believe he created us and loves us all, including you. When Adam and Eve sinned by disobeying God in the garden a wall was put up between God and man because God is Holy and can't bear sin or disobedience. He is, after all, the creator and we are the creation. Ever since, we have had an element of sinfulness in this world. All of us are born with that sinful nature and are separated from God.

Because He loves us so much, He came to earth in the form of a man whose name was Jesus. Jesus only lived 33 years and was executed by the Roman government. He WAS innocent. There were other men executed the same day, with Jesus. One of them laughed at Jesus and told him that if he was God, he ought to save their lives. But the other man told him to be quiet. Then that third man did something wonderful... instead of asking for his life to be saved, he admitted that he was there because of something he had done wrong. He confessed his sin and asked Jesus to remember him. Jesus told the man he would go to Heaven with him THAT DAY.

Robert, no one can force you and God will not make you, make a choice that you don't want to make. You can choose to deny that you have done wrong or you can admit that you are a sinner and ask Jesus to remember you and forgive you. He already did— when Jesus died that day, He said, "It is finished," meaning the wall had been torn down and man was no longer separated from God. The blood he shed covers our sins so we can be with God. If you choose, you will spend eternity in hell— hell being separated from God and it is a real place where people are consumed with the fire of guilt and hopelessness... FOREVER not 13 years or "life" but FOREVER. You can choose to ask for God's forgivingness for what you've done and give him your life. You will be met in heaven, I'm almost certain, by a 51 pound, brown haircd, brown-eyed girl named Cary Ann. She will walk up to you, and tell you again that God loves you. And you can make it "right" before you die by telling me and your own family that you are sorry.

No one can make you do this. And no one, not your lawyers, not anyone can stop you from doing this. If you prefer, you may write or speak to me through a media person. Paul Tinkle [radio broadcaster and station manager] from Martin has sent you a letter asking to meet with you. He has assured you and me that he will not edit your comments and will print exactly what you say. If you wish to meet with me, you must add me to your approved visitor's list and request this. If not, I will see you at 1 a.m. on October 19, 10 days after what would have been Cary Ann's 29th birthday.

I pray you make the right decision. Your daughter will also have to continue to live with knowing you've never expressed any regret for what you've done and you will forever be perceived as the "muster."

Charlotte Stout (Cary's mother)

The *Sun* printed Coe's unedited reply to Stout six days later.

Mrs. Stout,

I got your letter today, October 13. I read all your letter and hope you will read all of mine. Stories, as you said get altered and changed and don't always reflect the truth. The media says whatever will sell, no matter to the families feelings. First of all, I have never bragged about killing your daughter to become "famous." People tend to say things about me which isn't true, because of the nature of this charge. It (this charge) brings the worst out of people and no matter what I say or do, its bent the wrong way. I may be perceived as a "monster" by you and everyone else, but I am not. If you truly believe in God, then pray you can open your mind and let you see the truth. Its out there for anyone to see, if only they look. I did not kill your daughter and that's the truth. I will probably die here and have no reason to lie, and would you like to know why? I just don't have the will to go on living. My life has been a long road of pain and I do look forward to the end. I do truely feel sorry for you, but only God can help you or me right now. [TBI lead investigator] Alvin Daniel is your monster and mine. He lied and lied about everything. It's all in the records for anyone to see. Would you be willing to see it? Mrs. Stout, I know you want the real killer locked up. I'm not asking for myself, but for my family. Their lives have also been destroyed. I want you to check into this, in every case when someone on death row has been completely proven they aren't guilty and are set free, the state prosicuters and law enforcement have never admitted they were wrong! There's no doubt in my mind the state is going to murder me and I will have to face God for a lot of things, but this crime isn't one of them. If you want to visit me before I die, I will set it up. I am not mad at you, I just wish you could look more closely at the facts of this case before you write me off as a cold blooded monster. I haven't been talking to any press because they don't care about justice for us. I get so mad whenever some terrible crime happens, or a lot of people have been killed and the media pushes a mike and camera into the faces of people who have lost loved ones and says, "How do you feel at this very moment"! Just like they have been doing to you. I do see the pain in your eyes, but they only see a story. If you are wiling, why don't you go to my lawyer and tell them to "prove" to you that I'm not guilty. It won't take that much of your time and won't effect my outcome either way. My end is near and certain people will meake sure I'm murdered to keep me quite no matter what anyone says.

    May you find peace,

    Robert Glen Coe

Chapter 11:
Eleventh Hour

Don't ask me how this story ends. You know. And
each time the telling feels like a sinking in.

Joel Peckham, "Mud Season"

Riverbend staff had rehearsed the execution night
protocol many times, as required by law. Coe is awakened
at 6 a.m. of the appointed day. He visits with family and
lawyers and clergy during the day and is served his last meal
(Coe had already chosen the menu— fried catfish, french
fries, cole slaw, white beans, pecan pie, and sweet tea— and
made his funeral arrangements).

At midnight, the condemned man dresses in cotton
trousers, a t-shirt, and socks or cloth house shoes. Warden
Ricky Bell then reads his death warrant aloud. At 12:59 a.m.
guards ask him to step to the door of his cell to be handcuffed.
Coe is then asked to kneel on his bed while uniformed
guards prepare to hoist him onto a cross-like gurney. If Coe
refuses to cooperate, the specially-trained "extraction team"
will remove him bodily and strap him onto the gurney.

The team then wheels Coe the fifty feet from the Death
Watch Cell to the execution chamber. Dead man rolling. The
gurney is bolted to the chamber floor and an IV technician
inserts a catheter into each of Coe's arms (one to carry out the
actual execution and the other a reserve in case the primary
line fails), attaches tubing and then begins a saline drip. This
is standard medical procedure: connections must be clear,

ensuring that the chemicals do not mix in the IV lines and occlude the needle, preventing the drugs from reaching the inmate and botching the execution.

At approximately 1 a.m., Warden Ricky Bell and Prison Chaplain Bainbridge will join Coe in the chamber, whereupon Coe will be allowed to make a last statement and to pray with the chaplain. Then somewhere outside the chamber, a second technician will load the deadly chemicals into lethal injection syringes— the fast-acting barbituate *sodium pentathol* to render Coe unconscious, *curonium bromide* to slowly asphyxiate him, and *potassium chloride* to still his heart and send him into cardiac arrest. A heart monitor will be attached to Coe so that Riverbend officials can ascertain when death has occurred, usually within seven minutes of the injection.

Warden Ricky Bell said that when he first assumed the post he didn't think there'd ever be an execution at Riverbend. "But I realized many years ago that I would be involved in that process if I came here. It's the facility designed by the Department of Corrections to carry out executions. I'm prepared to do that," Bell said. "I don't let my personal feelings get involved. It's the job. It's my responsibility when it comes time to carry out the sentence. Personally, I dealt with this a while ago. Any views I may have… It goes with the turf. We do it and move on."

*

The federal public defender's office was still hoping Bell's original hunch was right. On October 11, 1999, the Tennessee Supreme Court granted Coe's motion and stayed his execution while his attorneys asked the United States

Supreme Court to reconsider his appeal of his original conviction, but by December 15, 1999, the state court had a new execution date, March 23, 2000, and ordered Shelby County Criminal Court Judge John Colton to hold and conclude a new mental competency hearing by February 9th in order to determine whether Coe understood that he was going to be executed and the reason why. Coe's attorneys had argued successfully that in previous mental competency hearings the burden had been Coe's to prove that he was not mentally fit to stand trial when it should have been the state's burden to prove he was competent. So in late January 2000, Coe returned to court for the first time since 1996, to the Memphis courtroom where he'd first been convicted nineteen years earlier.

Coe's behavior on the third day of the competency proceedings seemed so crazed that prosecution witness Dr. Daryl Matthews, a Hawaiian psychiatrist, considered it all a performance (a charge that had dogged Coe since his first trial). For nearly two hours, Coe screamed profanity and spat at Colton, prosecutors, reporters, and a half dozen courtroom security personnel who moved in to subdue him. "I told you I don't want to be here," Coe screamed, "take me back to Riverbend." He taunted assistant Attorney General Glenn Pruden by singing "Dear Pruden" to the tune of the old Beatles song "Dear Prudence." Each time his own attorney Robert Hutton attempted to proceed, Coe would launch into another minutes-long, profanity-laced tirade. "Judge Nixon's gonna overturn everything y'all do," he shouted at Judge Colton. "You ain't got no power."

Colton was determined to protect Coe's due process right to be present at all hearings regarding his case, and to follow state supreme court guidelines for such hearings which stipulated the defendant's presence, so during a lunch break he ordered Coe be wheeled into chambers and gagged with surgical gauze. Coe spat out the gauze in short order. "You can put all the restraints on me you want," Coe shouted at the bench. "I can still holler."

The judge then ordered bailiffs to tape Coe's mouth shut with adhesive tape and when he began to thrash to bind his hands and feet. Colton was ultimately forced to remove Coe from the courtroom and have him watch the proceedings on closed-circuit television. Newspapers the next morning ran a photo of the bound and gagged Coe, looking eerily like Hannibal Lecter, easily the most monstrous image of Coe to date.

Matthews called Coe's behavior "obviously a motivated, voluntary, conscious, highly manipulative display." Hadn't he claimed to his wife before his original trial that he could wrap any psychiatrist around his finger? In an earlier interview with Matthews, Coe was to have said that he was tired of hearing himself referred to as crazy and saw no advantage to a finding of incompetence anyway. "If they find you crazy, they keep you drugged up," he explained to Matthews, "but if they say you're well, they kill you." Matthews had learned that before Coe launched into one of his tirades that afternoon, the condemned man had turned to the Stout family and said to Charlotte, "I ain't doing this to disrespect y'all." This was clear evidence, according to prosecutors, that he was a deliberate decision-maker, almost cagey enough to fool seasoned attorneys, certainly competent to stand trial.

But Robert Hutton, who'd joined the defense team only in December, called the display more evidence of Coe's insanity. Defense expert William Keaner argued, when questioned by Hutton, that Coe displayed three radically different behaviors during the three days of the hearing, three formal and discrete personalities that appeared when Coe was confronted with stress. The stress of execution, he predicted, would cause Coe's psyche to fragment totally.

Colton ruled on February 2nd that Coe was fit for trial, and the defense team appealed in vain. The Tennessee State Supreme Court then upheld Colton's finding 4-1 that Coe had received a fair hearing in January and understood his crime and punishment. From late February to mid-May Coe's attorneys unleashed a barrage of motions, appeals and petitions at both the state and federal levels, enduring rejection after denial after rejection.

Besides the competency appeal, they'd filed an application for clemency with the governor's office, the goal a new hearing with the state's parole board. The application included a thirty-minute video, later shown on cable access channels in Nashville, showcasing interviews with Coe and his siblings, which the defense hoped would serve to re-humanize Coe. The clemency application also contained affidavits from three jurors from Coe's original 1981 trial who now preferred Coe spend life behind bars rather than be executed, and testimony from doctors concerning his mental state.

*

In the last month of his life, Robert Glen Coe was moved the short distance from Riverbend's Death Row— D Pod, Unit 2— to the Death Watch Cell in the Capital Punishment Unit of Building Eight a total of three times.

Each time was to be his last walk on prison grounds, his last breaths of fresh air.

Coe had grown accustomed. Despite the constant presence of corrections officers outside his eighty-square-foot Death Watch Cell, recording his every move in a smear-proof logbook, and the knowledge that the death chamber lay just fifty feet away, Robert Glen Coe saw the benefits of moving to Death Watch: he did not have to endure the taunts and threats of the other inmates, and the food was certainly better. He often enjoyed a breakfast of scrambled eggs, grits, toast with apple butter, cereal with milk, and coffee, and he loved fried bologna sandwiches and vanilla ice cream (all he cared to eat) later in the day. Coe also had unlimited phone privileges. While he sometimes spoke with his family, he usually called his lawyers to discuss his appeals.

Under an order of execution since May of 1999, Coe had begun to request dozens of court documents and called the public defenders office several times a day, showing more interest in his case, his attorneys say, than he had in the eighteen years since his original conviction. On the one hand, he sensed his death might indeed be near, but on the other Judge John Nixon's intercessions seemed to give him newfound hope. He'd become close with the receptionist at the public defender's office, a woman who'd once been terrified of him. They exchanged jokes and cards, full of gallows humor.

In the end, it was Judge Nixon's refusal to hear one of Coe's final appeals that seemed to signal the end. At 65, and under tremendous public pressure, Nixon had taken "senior status" as a trial judge, a sort of semi-retirement, and passed the case to newly-appointed judge Aleta Trauger, known for her independence but also her adherence to the letter of the law. It was Trauger's first capital case at any level and she stayed the execution on March 20, 2000, three days before Coe had been scheduled to die, citing doubts about the procedure used to determine Coe's mental competence. But Trauger lifted the stay on March 29, having found nothing in Judge John Colton's administration of the January competency hearing in Memphis "so offensive to existing precedent, so devoid of record support, or so arbitrary" as to merit overruling him.

When Coe's family gathered at the Riverbend prison on April 18th to see him for their third obligatory final family visit, they sensed something was different.

"Do you think this is it?" Coe asked Billie Jean. "Tell me the truth."

"Yeah, I believe this is it," his sister told him.

Coe's face reddened and he brought his shackled hands to his eyes. He was an innocent man, he said, but he was still sorry for the pain he'd caused them.

His sisters hushed him. They were sorry they hadn't visited more often.

Coe urged them not to watch the execution, but they insisted. They said they wanted to be the last faces he saw.

Bonnie and Billie Jean, Jimmy and his wife Frances, had been gathered in the Riverbend Death Watch visitation area since 11 a.m., seated on red plastic chairs. Coe, cuffed and shackled, sat between his sisters. These visits were never easy for Bonnie, who hyperventilated as she got closer to the prison and always brought a paper bag inside with her.

Then it was time. At 2:42 p.m., the guard stationed in the visiting room herded Coe's loved ones out, as they hurried to say everything in their hearts. They loved Robert Glen Coe, and forgave him, and believed in his innocence.

"Tell all your kids," Coe said. "Tell Jerry Wayne, tell Rebecca, tell Bubba. Tell them goodbye. Tell them, 'I love you.'"

There was a last ditch, a Hail Mary. Late that afternoon, local civil rights attorney George Barrett, acting on behalf of a cadre of prominent Nashville attorneys, joined the defense team to open a new front in the case. He argued that the techniques the Department of Corrections was planning to use to kill Coe were illegal and inhumane, put together by prison staff who were not medical professionals and could not possibly have known what they were doing. In effect, he argued, Warden Ricky Bell had prescribed these deadly drugs without a license. Bell admitted he'd merely visited prisons in Indiana and Texas to learn the amounts of the deadly chemicals to inject into Coe's body. The state's inexperience with executions was rearing its head again.

Davidson County circuit court judge Thomas Brothers agreed to hear the petition and attorneys for both sides waited outside his courtroom for an hour and a half, cell phones to their ears, while the judge deliberated. He emerged around 9 p.m. to say he was granting a stay of execution, the third in a month. "I'm really plowing new ground here," Brothers said, but he believed it "wrong that a group of laypeople got together and decided similar doses used in other cases would be used to kill Coe." Expertise was crucial and botched executions were a real concern. The chemicals had to be released into Coe's body sequentially to achieve the desired effect: the barbituate, administered first, should relax the body and minimize the effects of the two poisons that follow.

The injection of a highly-concentrated solution of potassium chloride, for instance, would be painful at the site of the I.V. line and all along that punctured arm if the muscle relaxing barbituate had not already rendered Coe unconscious.

The news of the stay surprised the defense team, though Coe's team did not believe the stay would be in place long. Prosecutors were already challenging both the timing of the filing and Judge Brothers's jurisdiction in the matter.

*

Charlotte Stout and her family were out to dinner in Nashville when they got word of the final stay. Charlotte and a large entourage— her husband and three grown sons, her mother, and a handful of others— had appeared at a memorial service for her daughter at 5:30 p.m. ("Poor Mr. Coe," she told the crowd, "my daughter has become a footnote in all this.") and then on a televison call-in show which aired on Nashville channel five (she'd made it a condition of her appearance that she not be asked to debate the merits of the death penalty). Lord, she kept thinking, I don't know if I can go through this again, just so Coe's lawyers can play more games.

The state mandated seven media witnesses be present at the execution, a pool to be chosen from applicants across the state. Paul Tinkle, of WCMT radio in Martin, who'd done play-by-play of my high school football games, had been chosen as the Weakley County representative. He'd asked his pastor, Brother Sing Oldham of the First Baptist Church, to accompany him to Nashville as his spiritual advisor. "I didn't know how I would deal with death— a planned death, a forced death," Tinkle said afterward.

He and Oldham left Martin for Nashville in the afternoon, stopping often to pray on the matter. They were stopped in the tiny town of Lobelville, Tennessee, when Tinkle got a phone call about the stay. "We didn't know if we were going to have to go all the way to the prison or not," Tinkle says. "We just kept driving and calling the Associated Press."

Tinkle and Oldham pulled into the press parking area at Riverbend prison in West Nashville at about 11:30 p.m. Outside the gates, 200 death penalty opponents, among them Sky McCracken and an Amnesty International official from Atlanta, commingled with forty death penalty supporters, including many whose family members had been murdered by one of the other 96 men on Riverbend's Death Row and wanted to see the execution floodgates opened as badly as the Amnesty official did not.

Oldham had not been invited to attend and so stayed with the car while Tinkle checked in. Before Tinkle went inside he had Oldham pray with him one last time, for strength, for Cary, and for Coe. There was a rumor making its way around the pressroom when he arrived that the Supreme Court was preparing to lift the stay. Tinkle saw Coe's sisters across the room and went to greet them. They were subdued. To compound their misery, Bonnie Deshields told Tinkle that her ex-husband and father of her children had been killed in a car accident in Hornbeak the day before.

At 12:45 a.m., just fifteen minutes before the execution was originally slated to begin, Department of Corrections spokesman Steve Hayes emerged from the prison to announce to the crowd of demonstrators that the stay had been lifted— the supreme court had confirmed the state's jurisdictional challenge— and that the execution would proceed as planned. "They seem hell bent on doing this," Sky McCracken told a *Jackson Sun* reporter.

Inside the prison waiting room, Ricky Bell delivered the same message to Coe's family. "Be strong," Bonnie Deshields told the others. "Everybody pray they don't botch it up."

Prison chaplain Frank Bainbridge prayed with the family before they left the waiting room to take their seats outside the death chamber. "Say a prayer for the rest of us," Paul Tinkle called to Bainbridge on behalf of the press corps, and he obliged. As her family filed out, Deshields thanked a female prison employee at the reception desk for all the kindness the woman had shown the family. "Bonnie, it's going to be okay," defense attorney Robert Hutton told her.

*

The Stout family arrived at the prison at midnight with Tennessee Highway Patrol escort. Charlotte Stout wondered what it would have been like to get stuck in traffic and miss the execution.

The execution was then delayed fifteen minutes by a technical problem, an issue with the closed-circuit cameras used to record the process. "Worked everyday in rehearsal for months," Mickey Stout later joked. Once that had been addressed, the families and prison officials were ushered into separate viewing areas— state law stipulated that families of the condemned and of the victim(s) view the execution from separate witness rooms, so a makeshift room was constructed for the Stout family.

When the curtain opened on the death chamber at 1:25 a.m., spectators saw Coe flat on his back on the gurney, arms and feet strapped. He was puffy, unshaven, pale from years spent largely indoors. "Short and pudgy," one reporter called him. A medical technician inserted the catheters in Coe's arms and started the saline drip at 1:20 a.m. Warden Bell stood at the head of the gurney and Chaplain Bainbridge at the foot, grasping Coe's left ankle in one hand and a Bible in the other. The room was brightly lit and miked, so spectators could hear what Coe said though he could not hear them. His loved ones signed to him (because his brother was deaf, they were all fluent).

Charlotte Stout said to Coe, "Never forget Cary's words, "Jesus loves you." It was her legacy, she said, to him and to her family, "and to us all."

Coe then offered his final statement.

"I love all of y'all with all my heart," he began, looking toward his family in the front row of the witness room. "I forgive the state of Tennessee for murdering me for something I didn't do, and that's God's truth."

He paused and addressed his alleged victim's mother. "Charlotte Stout, I forgive you, too, for helping the state murder me."

Bainbridge then led him in a recitation of The Lord's Prayer.

He looked at his family one final time. "Forgive everybody. God loves you," Coe said. "I'm gone. I'll see you in heaven. Bye-bye."

As the chemicals entered his body, around 1:30 a.m., witnesses say Coe jerked and then gasped once as if choking. But Paul Tinkle reported it was peaceful, like someone going to sleep. "God, forgive the state," yelled Bonnie Deshields.

"Oh, Lord! Oh, please help my baby brother," cried her

sister Billie Jean. "Please let it go fast, don't let it hurt."

Coe never moved again.

Charlotte Stout stared at Coe's body a long time, finally resting her head against the witness room glass. She thought to herself, "I've never looked at anybody before that I really and truly thought was not going to make it to heaven."

The curtain was closed at 1:36 a.m. in order for the Nashville Metro Medical Examiner to confirm the death. "He's resting now," Bonnie Deshields said. Curtain still closed, Warden Bell spoke from inside the chamber.

"Ladies and gentlemen, this concludes the legal execution of Robert Glen Coe. Time of death, 1:37 a.m. Please exit."

*

The Nashville *Tennessean* wrote that Coe met his end with dignity, something that had eluded him in life, that he seemed gentle. The man on the gurney bore no resemblance to the lunatic from that Memphis courtroom in January. Paul Tinkle said Coe seemed sane to him, "very much with it. He had total competence in everything he was talking about," Tinkle said.

Bonnie Deshields and her family declined to attend the post-execution press conference, but Charlotte Stout agreed to speak to the press. Prison personnel, having removed their nametags to avoid identification, escorted her and the media representatives into a foggy, chilly prison courtyard.

"It is finished," she began. "My daughter can rest," she said several times. "God created the judicial system to protect us from ourselves when we cannot protect ourselves from each other."

Reporters asked her about Coe's family. "This is a solemn

occasion and I don't take it lightly," Mrs. Stout continued. "My heart goes out to his family. My prayers are with them."

One reporter asked Charlotte Stout about Coe's failure to express remorse.

"Mickey warned me when I wrote him back in October that he would never apologize. Robert Glen Coe chose to kidnap, rape, and kill my daughter Cary. He chose his path. It is disappointing for him that he did not express remorse. That was his choice. I had hoped that Cary Ann would be meeting him in heaven. I am sure that she is quite saddened.

"That was his final way of hurting me," Mrs. Stout said, "because he knew that was all I wanted [an admission of guilt], so that was his only way of hurting me. For a split second it just kind of took me back, but the reality of it made me very, very sad for him."

Epilogue:
Time, Release

And you may find yourself in another part of the world… And you may find yourself in a beautiful house, with a beautiful wife, and you may ask yourself, "Well, how did I get here?"

Talking Heads, "Once in a Lifetime"

Sky McCracken stayed in Nashville with Coe's sisters the night of the execution in a safehouse provided by a local anti-death penalty group, rising early to drive them three hours home to West Tennessee through a thick fog that lay in the creek bottoms along Highway 22. They stopped part way home to fill the tank and saw that the *Commercial Appeal* had gone to press before the Supreme Court had lifted Judge Brothers's stay. "Coe Execution Stayed" read the headline, like the Dewey/Truman gaff. Insult to grievous injury.

The family held a one-hour memorial service for Robert Glen Coe a week later outside the tiny town of McKenzie. More than thirty relatives and friends gathered in a small country church where Coe's sisters placed their brother's ashes at the foot of the pulpit, flanking them with a framed grade school photo of Robert and a more recent shot of the grown Coe in the arms of family.

"He knew we loved him," Bonnie Deshields told the crowd, "We'll miss him with all our hearts."

The Reverend Sky McCracken said Coe was now beyond all fear, all pain, all confusion. "I am sure Robert was not comfortable with his soul in this world," McCracken said from the pulpit. "But I am sure he is well with it now."

Billie Jean Mayberry spoke of the shunning they'd endured as Coe's family, the pain of watching their brother die. It was different when their mother Annabelle died the year before after a long illness. Those last moments with their brother were the hardest 45 minutes of their lives. Knowing the appointed hour, says Camus, is the true cruelty of a public execution.

The Coe family continues to campaign against the death penalty, as spokespeople for organizations like Murder Victims' Families for Human Rights. "We don't want another state killing," Deshields said.

The family buried Coe's ashes in a secret family plot.

*

Charlotte Stout says stepping out of Riverbend prison the morning of the execution was eerie. A thick fog had rolled in and surrounded the prison's barbed fences, but in the courtyard where she and her family gathered she looked up and saw a crystal clear sky and heard songbirds, at 2 a.m. "It's over!" she thought to herself. "I can let it go forever. I don't have to worry anymore about what he's going to pull now or what his lawyers are up to. I don't have to deal with him anymore, forever!"

"Now you can get your life back," Charlotte's mother Joan Ogle told her. Coe had controlled her life for 21 years, Charlotte said, their vacations and time off from work revolving around appeals and hearings. Now it was over.

"We've been peaceful since Coe was executed," Charlotte told a *Jackson Sun* reporter by phone in the months that followed. "We're resting and Cary is resting. I feel safer for all of the children because there is one less person out there trying to hurt them."

"We're doing fine," Mickey Stout told the same reporter, though he says it's still hard to find himself in a conversation with a young person only to realize he or she is the same age Cary would be had she lived.

"Folks, this is wrong," Stout had told that U.S. House committee back in 1997, "I'm working, paying taxes, doing what I'm supposed to, and I get nothing." Charlotte Stout never did finish her book about Cary's life, lupus having robbed her of the energy to undertake a project like that. The last time I was in Greenfield I took a drive to the Stout home on Belair Drive. From a few houses away (as close as I dared go), I saw two signs posted on the lawn: one read "No Trespassing" and the other "For Sale." The real estate listing called the A-frame home "Greenfield's best kept secret!"

*

To the victors, the spoils. Original Coe prosecutor David Hayes became a circuit court of appeals judge and then a court of criminal appeals judge installed at Jackson, his colleague Leland McNabb a partner in a large Memphis firm that bears his name and a former president of the Memphis Bar Association. Each lists the Coe conviction prominently on his resume.

Coe's original court-appointed attorney, Max Speight, was sentenced in April of 2008 to eight years in state prison for bilking clients out of more than a million dollars. The original trial attorney, James O. Marty, Esquire, has been sanctioned several times by the Tennessee Bar for misconduct.

An article featuring the work of one of Coe's federal public defenders, Kelley Martin, appeared in the *New York Times* in the summer of 2009. She'd also represented indigent Tennessee Death Row inmate Sedley Alley until Alley was executed in 2006, and she's still working to get DNA work done on some of the evidence in Alley's case, hoping for a posthumous exoneration which would pump up the wrongful conviction rate in capital cases now estimated at .5 percent. But she can't find a Tennessee media outlet willing to sign on as a media plaintiff— newsroom staff and budgets are dwindling and expensive investigative reporting is the first thing to go.

*

A story can have a kind of time-release effect. Decades after we've first read it, Andre Dubus says, a story can open us up, by cut or caress, to a new truth. As an undergraduate enrolled in a summer course in the short story, I read Frank O'Connor's classic "Guests of the Nation" about a naïve young IRA fighter named Bonaparte who, after becoming chummy with the British Army regulars he and his comrades have kidnapped, is ordered to take the two men out to the bog and shoot them. He does so merely dutifully and with great reluctance— he no longer considers these men enemies but friends— and afterward, with the two dead soldiers "stiffening into the bog," Bonaparte returns to the house where they'd kept the Brits and feels positively unmoored; "the birds and the bloody stars were all far away," he explains, "and I was somehow very small and very lost and lonely like a child astray in the snow. And anything that happened to me afterwards, I never felt the same about again."

As I was simultaneously enrolled in a philosophy course that summer, I wrote a critical essay arguing that the O'Connor story was an existentialist tour de force, a response which seems perfectly adequate considering my age and experience. But the story has stayed with me, and now I read it differently, feel it differently. I have felt the existential abandonment Bonaparte feels when none of the explanations offered soothe, when none of culture's big abstractions seem worth killing or dying for.

I must say I don't share Charlotte Stout's conviction about the state of Robert Glen Coe's soul, or Sky McCracken's conviction on the matter either. I have a hard time believing God took Cary Ann so that her father would come home to Jesus, that Cary heard angels on her staircase days before she died, or that evil spirits entered Robert Glen Coe that day in Greenfield and compelled him to do the unspeakable. I don't believe in angels or evil spirits period, or the "face of evil" Weakley County Sheriff Mike Wilson says he saw on Coe that first day in court, though I do believe those are the kinds of ideas that get a man executed, the sentimental explanations that prevent us from looking very hard at the ignorance and injustice and inaction, what RFK called "the violence of institutions," that make crimes like Cary's murder inevitable. I saw it happen with my own two eyes, done in my name.

*

While researching this book, I maintained a file titled simply "Coincidence" which contained random connections I was discovering I had to the case. Many were admittedly trivial— that my mother had in 1979 (and for many years after) driven a Gran Torino like the one Coe drove the night of the murder, that my younger sister Ruth and Cary Ann shared not only a ballet class but also a birthday (October 9), that Coe was executed on my younger son's birthday (April 19), that I shared the killer's first name and the number on the football jersey Coe was wearing at the time of his arrest (50) was the number I had worn during my high-school football career. Interesting, yes, but coincidences to which only a nutty numerologist would assign real significance. Some of the other connections do seem truly meaningful, though. That I had known Cary, that Coe had been on Meek Street so near my own home the night before the murder, that so many of the other principals in the case, from attorneys to ministers to media representatives, are people I've known all my life, says something about life in "Happy Town, U.S.A", not only about how we were all affected by the crime but also how we all bear the responsibility for its disposition, no matter how many times Paul Tinkle asks that a clergyman pray for God's intercession. I think we'll carry it to our graves.

A year or two ago, I got an e-mail asking if I knew anyone interested in teaching in one of the prisons that dot the landscape of northern New York like Wal-Marts. I volunteered, at first going alone to a federal penitentiary to teach inmates to write their own stories, then, following the lead of a Temple University professor, bringing my undergraduate students along to a medium security state facility to learn alongside the incarcerated men.

Though they'd entered the prison with much trepidation, many of my students ultimately considered the class among their most powerful educational experiences. On the final visit the class made to the jail, more than one inmate talked about how, except for a few bad choices, we were all the same. The students nodded, though one young woman (I applaud her still for this) pointed in her term paper to the sentimentality of that idea, to all the reasons from race to class to geography that made such a comment untrue. Still she conceded that these were two groups— privileged white kids from a toney rural private university and (mostly) African-American cons from New York City— who likely would never have met otherwise, and that it was a powerful thing to cross the moat, to counteract so much of the social pressure that kept the groups apart. "When you teach a man to hate and fear his brother," RFK said in that speech to the Cleveland Club, "then you also learn to confront others not as fellow citizens but as enemies... to look at our brothers as aliens, men with whom we share a city, but not a community; men bound to us in common dwelling, but not in common effort."

And I finally had a good answer when one of the incarcerated men asked me what I was doing there. "What makes Professor Bob tick?" asked a man named Arthur Blake.

I told them about Billy Rex and Jerry Max Pickett, my father's courses at the Lake County prison when I was little, the Meek Streeters who ended up doing time there, about Cary Medlin and Robert Glen Coe.

Driving home in the white university van after our meetings, I was always full of gratitude for my students' courage, for the opportunity to experience something besides just another day at the office. Often I thought of Robert Glen Coe and Cary Ann Medlin, Cary's still the clearest, most plaintive voice in this old story, the voice of human mercy. Though when she speaks to me it's not of Jesus or the heaven that may await me. She holds me to account in this world: "Hey Bobby Cowser! What are you doing here?"

Also Available from UNO Press:

William Christenberry: Art & Family by J. Richard Gruber (2000)

The El Cholo Feeling Passes by Fredrick Barton (2003)

A House Divided by Fredrick Barton (2003)

Coming Out the Door for the Ninth Ward edited by Rachel Breunlin
   from The Neighborhood Story Project series (2006)

The Change Cycle Handbook by Will Lannes (2008)

Cornerstones: Celebrating the Everyday Monuments & Gathering Places of New Orleans
   edited by Rachel Breunlin, from The Neighborhood Story Project series (2008)

A Gallery of Ghosts by John Gery (2008)

Hearing Your Story: Songs of History and Life for Sand Roses by Nabile Farès
   translated by Peter Thompson, from The Engaged Writers Series (2008)

The Imagist Poem: Modern Poetry in Miniature edited by William Pratt
   from The Ezra Pound Center for Literature series (2008)

The Katrina Papers: A Journal of Trauma and Recovery by Jerry W. Ward, Jr.
   from The Engaged Writers Series (2008)

On Higher Ground: The University of New Orleans at Fifty by Dr. Robert Dupont (2008)

Us Four Plus Four: Eight Russian Poets Conversing translated by Don Mager (2008)

Voices Rising: Stories from the Katrina Narrative Project edited by Rebeca Antoine (2008)

Gravestones (Lápidas) by Antonio Gamoneda, translated by Donald Wellman
   from The Engaged Writers Series (2009)

The House of Dance and Feathers: A Museum by Ronald W. Lewis by Rachel Breunlin
   & Ronald W. Lewis, from The Neighborhood Story Project series (2009)

I hope it's not over, and good-by: Selected Poems of Everette Maddox by Everette Maddox (2009)

Portraits: Photographs in New Orleans 1998-2009 by Jonathan Traviesa (2009)

Theoretical Killings: Essays & Accidents by Steven Church (2009)

Voices Rising II: More Stories from the Katrina Narrative Project edited by Rebeca Antoine (2010)

Rowing to Sweden: Essays on Faith, Love, Politics, and Movies by Fredrick Barton (2010)

Dogs in My Life: The New Orleans Photographs of John Tibule Mendes (2010)

Understanding the Music Business: A Comprehensive View edited by Harmon Greenblatt
   & Irwin Steinberg (2010)

The Fox's Window by Naoko Awa, translated by Toshiya Kamei (2010)

A Passenger from the West by Nabile Farés, translated by Peter Thompson
   from The Engaged Writers Series (2010)

The Schüssel Era in Austria: Contemporary Austrian Studies, Volume 18
   edited by Günter Bischof & Fritz Plasser (2010)

The Gravedigger by Rob Magnuson Smith (2010)

Everybody Knows What Time It Is by Reginald Martin (2010)

When the Water Came: Evacuees of Hurricane Katrina by Cynthia Hogue & Rebecca Ross
   from The Engaged Writers Series (2010)

Aunt Alice Vs. Bob Marley by Kareem Kennedy, from The Neighborhood Story Project series (2010)

Houses of Beauty: From Englishtown to the Seventh Ward by Susan Henry
   from The Neighborhood Story Project series (2010)

Signed, The President by Kenneth Phillips, from The Neighborhood Story Project series (2010)

Beyond the Bricks by Daron Crawford & Pernell Russell
   from The Neighborhood Story Project series (2010)

New Orleans: The Underground Guide by Michael Patrick Welch & Alison Fensterstock (2010)

unopress.org